BROKEN BREAD
AND BROKEN BODIES

BROKEN BREAD
AND BROKEN BODIES

THE LORD'S SUPPER
AND WORLD HUNGER

Joseph A. Grassi

ORBIS BOOKS
Maryknoll, New York 10545

The Catholic Foreign Mission Society of America (Maryknoll) recruits and trains people for overseas missionary service. Through Orbis Books Maryknoll aims to foster the international dialogue that is essential to mission. The books published, however, reflect the opinions of their authors and are not meant to represent the official position of the society.

Copyright © 1985 by Joseph A. Grassi

Published by Orbis Books, Maryknoll, NY 10545 221694
Manufactured in the United States of America

New Testament biblical quotations are from the Revised Standard Version
Old Testament biblical quotations are from the New American Bible, © 1970 by
the Confraternity of Christian Doctrine, Washington, D.C.

Library of Congress Cataloging in Publication Data

Grassi, Joseph A.
  Broken bread and broken bodies.

  Bibliography: p.
  Includes index.
  1. Lord's Supper. 2. Jesus Christ—Person and
offices. 3. Hunger—Religious aspects—Christianity.
I. Title.
BV825.2. G69   1985   261.8′3   84-18888
ISBN 0-88344-193-4 (pbk.)

Contents

Preface

The title *Broken Bread and Broken Bodies* is used to describe the primary contrasts in this book. Broken bread has become a significant symbol in Christian liturgy all over the world. Breaking bread as a liturgical symbol is repeated millions of times each year by hundreds of millions of Christians. The Lord's Supper bears symbolic and sacramental meaning, but at a more fundamental level it is simply a sharing of food.

Although the Eucharist has many shades of meaning, they all flow from the central belief that it is a special way that Jesus wished to be remembered. This "remembering" is much more than a nostalgic or emotional recollection. It is a public pledge of imitation and discipleship. In eating broken bread, Christians pledge to become like Jesus: to assimilate his lifestyle and obey his word. Food for the hungry was so important to Jesus that Matthew's Gospel presents this concern among Jesus' last words before the passion account: "I was hungry and you gave me food." This phrase and a variant are stated four times in the same scene (Matt. 25:35, 37, 42, 44) and thus take on great importance, for in the semitic mentality importance was stressed by repetition. During Eucharist celebrations and in private prayer Jesus' own prayer, the Our Father, is solemnly recited, including its petition "give us this day our daily bread." It is essential that both aspects of the broken bread be remembered: it is a symbol of spiritual nourishment, and it is a call for actual food for the hungry.

Yet the stark reality of world hunger and broken bodies stands in glaring contrast to this broken bread of the Eucharist. It is estimated that about fifteen million people die of starvation each year. More than five hundred million people suffer from acute hunger and severe malnutrition. This occurs despite the fact that there is sufficient food to feed them and enough land to raise the necessary crops (see Toton, part 1). Unnecessary suffering and death confront us. What can one person do about all of this? We often feel a sense of discouragement and isolation when we give serious thought to the problem. At times we may give donations of money and food for the hungry, yet we often come away with a sense of guilt that we have done too little in the face of a global problem.

The purpose of this book is to point out how a deep understanding of and participation in the Eucharist can mobilize effective individual and community action to start a great miracle of sharing that will lead to the end of hunger. The book will show how a meaningful celebration of the Supper of the Lord can lead to political and social action to eliminate poverty and oppression—the root causes of world hunger. Part 1 is entitled "The Eucharist and Radical Discipleship." The Eucharist is deeply rooted in the baptismal pledge of obedience to Christ. This obedience is expressed through a commitment to imitate his lifestyle of service to the hungry and poor. Part 2 is entitled "The Eucharist/Last Supper: Sacrament and Action—Sign of the Kingdom." It stresses the connection between the Eucharist as sacrament and human liberation. This connection can serve as an important catalyst of an effective movement to end the terrible scourge of world hunger.

PART I

THE EUCHARIST AND
RADICAL DISCIPLESHIP

Introduction to Part I

At the very core of the Eucharist is a solemn pledge or covenant to be a disciple of Jesus, to imitate his lifestyle. This brings the Eucharist into the practical spheres of everyday life. The connection between the Eucharist and discipleship is found within the meaning of baptism. While baptism is the first initiation into Christian life, the Eucharist is a continual renewal of this commitment. One of the earliest explanations of baptism is found in Romans 6:1–18. Here, in verse 17, Paul speaks of a "rule of teaching" *(typon didachēs)* to which Christians have committed themselves. This "rule of teaching" made very definite demands on their behavior and actions. Writing to the Galatians, Paul states,

> All of you who have been baptized into Christ have clothed yourselves with him. There does not exist among you Jew or Greek, slave or freeman, male or female. All are one in Christ Jesus [3:27–28].

To be clothed with Christ is to identify with him and imitate him. When through baptism people are clothed in Christ, the forces that segregate individuals and groups are opposed. This breaks down racial barriers between Jew and Greek, sexual inequality between man and woman, and class barriers between slaves and free persons. The Eucharist is a renewal of the baptismal commitment to imitate Jesus and break those barriers.

Because of the importance of practicing discipleship to Jesus in a concrete way, early Christian teachers pointed out a very specific way of life and behavior that could be followed by the newly baptized. One of the earliest Christian documents, the first letter to the Thessalonians, (ca. A.D. 49–50) states that early Christians

3

learned their new way of life by imitating the "little church" composed of Paul and his companions. Paul wrote, "Now, my brothers, we beg and exhort you in the Lord Jesus that even as you learned from us how to conduct yourselves in a way pleasing to God—which you are indeed doing—so you must learn to make still greater progress" (1 Thess. 4:1).

Paul was deeply convinced of the connection between the Eucharist and imitation of Jesus. On one occasion, Paul sharply criticized Corinthian Christians' celebration of the Lord's Supper because they had disregarded poor and hungry community members. He wrote: "What I have to say is not in praise, because your meetings are not profitable but harmful" (1 Cor. 11:17). When Paul wrote this statement, he was very conscious of the biblical prophetic tradition that worship without justice is a sham and an insult to a God of justice.

At the essence of the Eucharist lies a renewal of the baptismal covenant to follow Jesus; even as far as death. The eating of bread, his body, is an act of assimilation and identity. We do become the food we eat, if we really digest it and make it part of ourselves. To accentuate this assimilation and imitation as aspects of discipleship, the Wisdom teachers of the Bible explained discipleship through the symbols of eating and drinking. In the book of Proverbs, Divine Wisdom invites people to become disciples by declaring, "Come eat of my food, and drink of the wine I have mixed" (9:5-6).

In order to understand fully the Eucharist and discipleship to Jesus, we must first understand his life. To do that we must know something of the world in which he lived. Part 1 of this book thus contains a survey of pertinent social, economic, political, and religious forces at work in Israel at the time of Jesus' life. Part 1 also focuses upon Jesus' commands about discipleship and examines the relationship between discipleship and the central theme of Jesus' life—service to the poor, the hungry, the oppressed.

Chapter 1

Israel in Jesus' Time:
Oppression and Stratification

Today there is a widespread feeling, especially among young people, that the world is headed for catastrophe and destruction. Only in this light can the political views and behavior of these young people be understood. Likewise, we can better understand Jesus when we recover his sense of impending disaster and observe how this affected everything he did. In his book *Jesus before Christianity* Albert Nolan writes:

> Very many Jews at that time were convinced that the world was on the brink of an apocalyptic catastrophe. It was in view of this catastrophe . . . and in terms of his own understanding of it that Jesus set out on his mission. With what I would like to call an unparalleled leap of creative imagination, this man saw a way out, and even more than a way out—he saw the way to total liberation and fulfillment for mankind [8].

POLITICAL, SOCIAL, AND ECONOMIC SOURCES OF OPPRESSION

In Jesus' time there were sound bases for a sense of impending catastrophe and for a desire for liberation. The land of Israel was seething with injustice that resulted in acute suffering for a large segment of the population (see Cassidy). If one were to have asked the people in the street what the cause of this was, they would have answered without hesitation: first of all the hated foreign oppressor, Rome. Israel had lost its independence in 64 B.C. when Pompey established Rome's control by a military victory. At first Herod the Great, as a puppet king, ruled the land for Rome until his death in 6 B.C. Then his son Herod Antipas was installed as tetrarch of Galilee in the north and Peraea on the Jordan's east bank. Another son, Archelaus, received Judea, Samaria, and Idumea. However, after nine years Rome decided to place the latter areas under the direct control of a Roman governor.

Rome had no policy of helping "developing countries." The provinces were exploited for the security and enrichment of the imperial government. The emperor awarded governorships as special political plums to faithful political or military leaders. These men looked forward to such positions as a reward for their service and as an opportunity to amass an abundant "retirement fund." The means to obtain this was a system of excessive assessments and taxation.

Throughout the empire, the Roman system of taxation was carefully organized. There were three types of taxes: first, a land tax payable in produce or money; second, a poll tax on everyone except the children and the elderly; finally, market sales taxes, tolls, and custom duties on imports and exports. The tax burden was made unbearable by the fact that the position of tax collector was sold to the highest bidders. This meant that tax collection was a business, and tax collectors were notorious for their ability to overcharge the people and thus get a better return on their investment. Tax collectors were a wealthy group. They used their Roman connection to amass fortunes, a large part of which was obtained through overcharging and injustice. Luke singles out Zacchaeus, "a chief tax collector and a wealthy man" (Luke 19:2). He is considered a "sinner" by the people (Luke 19:7). When people failed to pay taxes to such men, they were imprisoned or otherwise severely punished by the Roman military.

The second cause of oppression was the greedy rule of the Herods and their families. This was felt especially in Galilee, where most of Jesus' ministry took place. Herod the Great's family had acquired a large proportion of the rich agricultural land of Galilee—Herod probably owned from one-half to two-thirds of all the land, some of which was acquired by direct confiscation. This limited most farmers to small plots from which they obtained barely enough to subsist. Others could only look for work as day-laborers, whose wages were very low and by no means secured. The parable of the workers in the vineyard illustrates their plight. In the story the day-workers are ready for work at dawn, but only some of them are hired. Others are still waiting at midmorning, noon, and late afternoon. The result is that some, even if hired, will not receive the day's wage needed for bare subsistence (Matt. 20:1-10). This oppressive and unjust system was perpetuated by landowners like the Herods. Taxes in Israel under the Herods were even more oppressive than those under Rome. It has been estimated that the Jews in Galilee paid between 30 and 40 percent of their income to government and religious taxes (Cassidy, 192). The tax burden was so severe that the Jews requested that Galilee be placed under direct Roman rule.

The third source of oppression was the wealthy Israelite landowners. Many of these were from the limited number of families from which Rome appointed the high priests. Because the high priests had control of the temple area, they also profited by the income from business conducted there. This profit was in addition to the ordinary priestly income from the sacrifices and offerings made in the Temple. Because it was to their economic advantage, the rich Jewish families were very much in favor of maintaining the status quo vis-à-vis Rome.

The suffering caused by these oppressive forces was immense. Because the basis of the economy was agricultural and because the rural economic system was so unjust, a large part of the population lived in extreme poverty and suffering. Those who suffered the most from the situation were those who were marginalized even from the agricultural system: widows, orphans, strangers, and the sick. In the Bible these are the people who suffer most from oppression.

Besides resulting in widespread suffering among the rural population and the marginalized, the dominant system severely oppressed women and brought about a terribly unjust distribution of economic and social benefits among classes.

From a social viewpoint, the most obvious inequality in first-century Israel was the distinctly inferior position held by women in that society. Like many other ancient societies, the Jewish society of Jesus' day was patriarchal. Women were placed in a subordinate position both in the family and in public life. Until a daughter was married, she was considered as part of the father's family property and household. He could either accept or reject any proposals of marriage for his daughter, although she would have to concur in his decision. After marriage the woman fell under the jurisdiction of her husband. Any contracts or vows she made had to be approved by him. It was hoped that the woman would give birth within a short time to a son, an heir. If she did not, she was blamed and very often divorced. It was a male prerogative to divorce—a decision based on property rights. A woman could not divorce her husband except under very unusual circumstances. If a husband died, the woman's position often deteriorated. If there were sons, they received all the family property. Neither the wife nor the daughters had any legal title to the inheritance unless there were no male heirs.

The system that oppressed women also fostered and attempted to justify a strict stratification of society along social, economic, religious, and ethnic lines. The rich were a special class who kept within their own company. They shied away from the poor but not without some sense of guilt. They could not go out on the streets without encountering the misery and suffering of the masses of Israel. The rich knew how much the poor resented their domination and held them responsible for economic injustice.

RELIGION AND STRATIFICATION

The religious institutions in first-century Israel worked to further segregate groups within society. At that time, writing and reading were not only skills but part of a profession limited to a small number of educated people, the scribes. In addition to writing, scribes had to know law, business, and civil and social contracts. Because the principal Hebrew book was the Bible, the scribe was usually a religious teacher as well. The laws of Moses found in the Bible were the dominant forces in daily Jewish life, and these laws were continually updated by application to every detail of life. Thus most ordinary people looked up to the scribe as a teacher of the Law and as a guide for their lives. As a result, the scribes perceived themselves as members of a superior class that held extensive knowledge of life and of the Law. In view of their training and education, many scribes looked down upon other professions. Sirach the Scribe, for instance, writes of artisans in this manner: "They do not occupy the judge's bench, nor are they prominent in the assembly; they set forth no decisions or judgments, nor are they found among the rulers" (38:33). This tendency toward haughtiness is echoed in the statement of the chief priests and Pharisees in John 7:48, "This crowd knows nothing about the law—and they are lost anyway!" Matthew's Gospel reports that Jesus criticized this attitude of some scribes. Matthew gives the examples of their concern to get the seats of honor at banquets and synagogues, to be greeted first on the streets, and to have the special title of "rabbi" or "teacher" (23:6–7).

While religious leaders perpetuated class distinctions, religious laws also caused or reinforced such divisions. Among these were laws about "clean" and "unclean" individuals. These laws had nothing to do with hygiene, except in a secondary sense. These distinctions were based upon actions or physical conditions that disqualified a person from public worship and contact with others in groups or social gatherings. These laws were usually not a matter of ethical evaluations of behavior. In fact, sometimes a virtuous action, commanded by the Law, would cause ritual uncleanness. For example, burial of the dead was commanded by the Law, but touching the dead made a person incur uncleanness for a period of time. There was also a large group of sicknesses that brought about uncleanness. Among these were some mental illnesses, which were commonly believed to be caused by a devil, who was an "unclean spirit" (Mark 1:23–28). Leprosy and various skin diseases also caused one to be labeled as unclean (Lev. 13). People so afflicted could never attend social or religious gatherings because some types of uncleanness were considered highly contagious.

Women were especially subject to being designated as ritually unclean because of their closeness to the powerful forces of life and fertility connected with blood. Women were "unclean" for seven days each month at the time of their menstruation. They were so "contagious" that even the furniture, dishes, or things they touched could convey this uncleanness to others (Lev. 17). They were unclean for forty days after the birth of a male child and eighty days after that of a female child. The desperate situation of some women with frequent or intermittent flow of blood is behind the story told in Mark 5:21–34 of the woman who is healed by Jesus. The inability to know whether a woman was subject to these "uncleannesses" was a factor in inhibiting men from talking to women in public, because this type of uncleanness was contagious. A detailed account of various types of uncleanness is found in Leviticus 11–15. Although not the direct intention of these laws, the segregation reinforced by them easily lent itself to discrimination and inequality.

The greatest area of social separation was in the relationships between Jews and Gentiles. There was a large Gentile population in Israel, especially in Galilee where there were a number of Greek cities. Yet the average Jew and Gentile were worlds apart. Many Gentiles considered Jews as very different and "strange" because of their exclusive monotheism and refusal to have any contact with other religions. Rigid Jewish food laws and fears of ritual uncleanness made any real fellowship between the two groups almost impossible. In addition, there was Jewish resentment toward most non-Jews as either being part of the foreign occupation of their country or as cooperators with Roman authority.

Thus in the Israel of Jesus' time, political, economic, social, and religious forces combined to create a highly stratified social order in which a small minority accumulated great wealth and the vast majority had almost nothing but suffering and hunger. It is by observing Jesus within this context that we can begin to discover the impact and meaning of Jesus' ministry. Jesus was a man of his times who took history seriously. Because he felt called to be a leader of his people, it is important to note how he perceived his role in light of the situation and needs of Israel. Did he consider himself as a purely spiritual leader, or did he see his mission as intimately interwoven with the political and social realities of his time? It is to this question that our next chapter addresses itself.

Chapter 2

Jesus: Spiritual Leader or Political and Social Revolutionary?

The quest for the meaning of Christianity in today's world begins with answering the question posed in the title of this chapter. Few have questioned that Jesus' leadership was rooted in his appreciation of the Spirit and grounded in the religious faith of Israel. Yet some Christians have found reason to believe in a "spiritual Jesus" whose effects are primarily interior and individual. To believe in such a Jesus is a limitation of faith. Basic to Christian faith is the belief that Jesus is a man. Being a man or a woman—an adult—means entering into relationships with people and the world. Jesus was a spiritual man and teacher, but, as a man, he also had deep relationships with other human beings and with the historical world in which he lived.

In his book *Following Jesus,* Segundo Galilea, a noted Latin American theologian, emphasizes the deep spiritual dimension of discipleship in Jesus' teaching. However, at the same time he makes the following statement:

> To situate authentically the mission of Christ in relation to the political situation of his time, we need to apply to this question the mystery of the Incarnation. To speak of a redemptive-historical Incarnation of the Son of God is not just to affirm that God became man at a determined and identifiable time and place. It is to affirm also that Jesus

11

came to participate in some way in the historical, religious, social, and political movements of his time and that these movements influenced and conditioned his activity [102–3].

To understand these movements and thus further to understand the social, political, and religious milieu in which Jesus preached and acted, it is first necessary to review the backgrounds and prototypes of these movements and their leaders.

GOD AND THE PROPHETS AS PROTOTYPAL LIBERATORS

God and the great prophetic leaders of the Old Testament served as prototypes of the kind of leader Jesus was to become—one sensitive to the historical situation of human beings and especially ready to serve the downtrodden. The Wisdom tradition is one of the ancient streams of thought in the Bible. It draws its material from sensitive, acute listening to people, as well as from observations of nature and the world. The Bible presents King Solomon in his early years as a model of the seeker of wisdom. On one occasion, the king had a dream in which God would grant him anything he wished. Solomon responded as follows:

> Give your servant, therefore, an understanding heart to judge your people and to distinguish right from wrong. For who is able to govern this vast people of yours? [1 Kings 5:9].

The Hebrew words that were translated as "understanding heart" mean literally "listening heart." Solomon asks for a listening heart because he knows that only a sensitive, open, and listening person will be able to serve others and find God in the world. In the case of Solomon, such a disposition would enable him to serve as king through a deep understanding of the needs of his people.

The model of a listening heart is actually based on God—the supreme and most sensitive listener to the needs of people. The book of Exodus presents God as a compassionate liberator coming down to take up a people's cause precisely because God has an acute sense of that people's suffering in Egypt. God appears to Moses in a burning bush on Sinai and says:

> I have witnessed the affliction of my people in Egypt and have heard their cry of complaint against their slave drivers, so I know well what they are suffering. Therefore I have come down to rescue them from the hands of the Egyptians [Exod. 3:7–8].

All sincere Jews read the Bible in order to imitate God, especially as God was known through works in their history. The supreme model for Jesus to imitate was God, his Father. Jesus would certainly have understood the words from heaven at his baptism, "You are my beloved Son" (Mark 1:11), as an invitation to radical obedience and imitation of his Father. We cannot imagine the beginning of Jesus' career except as a deep response to the needs of his people, a response modeled on God and Moses at the time of the Exodus from Egypt.

The liberation of Israel from Egypt was a political, social, and religious act. It was political in that the people were delivered from Egyptian domination to a land of their own. It was social in freeing them from slavery, from being members of the lowest oppressed class of Egyptian society. It was religious in leading them to Sinai and then to Israel where they could freely worship their God. When Moses first spoke to Pharaoh, the religious motivation to worship in freedom was primary. He said (in the name of God) to Pharaoh, "Let my people go, that they may celebrate a feast to me in the desert" (Exod. 5:1).

For Israel the memory of its escape from Egyptian oppression always constituted a model of liberation in future crises of history. The people of Israel could not divorce its religion from the nation, nor social conditions from its religious faith. Moses as a spiritual, social, and political leader became a model for future Jewish leaders that motivated not only Jesus but a variety of liberation movements during his time.

To answer the question posed in the title of this chapter, it is important to compare and contrast Jesus' ideas and actions with those of the members of religious parties and liberation movements of his time. Since the early 1960s the literature in this area has been growing (see Rhoads for a bibliography). Some of the principal results of this scholarship is summarized in the following section.

JESUS AND THE PALESTINE LIBERATION MOVEMENTS OF THE FIRST CENTURY

Jesus and all the Palestine liberation movements of his day held at least one thing in common: their basic faith in a God of history who was involved and acting in the events of their land and people. This belief contained a determined hope that no matter how desperate their present situation, God would, at some point, intervene to bring justice and end oppression. This future day of intervention was often called "the day of the Lord." The hope for this coming great intervention of God was based on the firm conviction that God had created humanity to be one great family living in peace, harmony, and justice. To effect this purpose, God had made a lasting covenant with Israel to be God's own people and a chosen instrument. This God, by nature, was a God of justice and history. God could not indefinitely allow the people of Israel to live in servitude and oppression. In the past God had intervened in Egypt and repeatedly throughout history. God would certainly do so again. Because their condition was so appalling and desperate, many people of Jesus' time felt that the appointed time could come at any moment.

These conditions generated a number of movements that challenged the dominant institutions and classes in first-century Palestine. From the years prior to Jesus' birth to the outbreak in A.D. 66 of the Jewish War with Rome, many local, often uncoordinated revolutionary groups sprang up in Palestine. In A.D. 6 there was a great revolt in Galilee led by Judas the Galilean. His actions and those of many of his descendants established a pattern for later revolutionary groups that followed in their footsteps. Most of Judas's followers were poor Galileans disenfranchised of their property and rights either by the Herod family, Rome, or rich Jewish landowners. These latter worked hand in hand with Rome or the Herods. Many of these landowners were from the rich priestly families from which Rome selected the Jewish high priests. These rich families formed a prominent ruling class that controlled the Sanhedrin, the governing body of the Jews, which cooperated with Rome. In Galilee the revolution led by Judas was directed against King Herod and his family as oppressors and principal landowners.

The Sicarii

One of the revolutionary groups patterned upon Judas's movement was the Sicarii. Like Judas's revolt, the roots and cause of the Sicarii movement were the oppressive social, political, economic, and religious forces in Galilee. The Sicarii first appeared as a coordinated party about the time of the outbreak of the Jewish War. The name *Sicarii* comes from the Latin *sicae* which means "daggers." These revolutionaries earned this name because they carried concealed daggers that they used for assassination, kidnapping, or other terrorist activities.

The Sicarii movement's motivation was in part religious. Absolute obedience to the first commandment forbade worship of strange gods and ordered the worship of only one God. For the Sicarii this meant revolt against Rome—which had attempted to impose its own religious practices—and trust in God to give them victory no matter how overwhelming the odds against them. The Sicarii movement was also political and messianic. Its members wished to restore the kingdom of David as promised in the scriptures. Consequently, the leaders posed as messiahs ready to liberate their people with God's help in the same way as did Moses. Most of these revolutionaries were also religious reformers. Some of them came from a radical wing of the Pharisees.

The Zealots

In contrast to the Sicarii, the Zealot movement was directed more against pagan culture than the imperial rule—although the Zealots saw Rome as embodying that culture. The Zealot goal was a holy war that would purify Israel by resisting all accommodation with Greek or Roman religious customs and practices. The Zealot ideal was a theocracy in which God ruled a pure Israel through holy priests. Although the Zealot movement had considerable influence and followers before the Jewish War, it only emerged as an organized party in A.D. 66. At that time, under the leadership of Eleazar, Zealots entered the Temple and prevented the priests from accepting any further offerings for sacrifice on the part of Romans and foreigners. The Zealots desired to purify the Temple from Gentile influence and eliminate the high priestly families that had cooperated with Rome. Thus the Zealot movement was not solely directed against Rome—it was also a revolt of lower class priests and peasants mainly from Judea against the dominating aristocracy of the high priestly and other rich ruling families. Within the movement there were apparently no messianic figures associated with the kingdom of David and its restoration. Like the Sicarii, the Zealot movement was a social, religious, and political revolution.

The Pharisees

The Pharisaic ideal was to place every detail of daily life under the Law and thus under obedience to God. The Pharisees were a very easily identified group. They had regular meetings and welcomed others to join them once they showed the same zeal for the Law and its observances. In daily life they were characterized by their scrupulous adherence to every detail of the Law. For example, while ordinary people would pay the required tithes ordered by the Law—this usually interpreted to be a tenth of wine, grain, and oil—the Pharisees paid a tenth of *everything*, even garden herbs and seeds (see Matt. 23:33; Luke 18:12). In addition, they felt that all Israel, not only the priests, were a priestly people—Exodus 10:6 calls Israel a "kingdom of priests." Consequently, they kept all the biblical laws including those that were written only for priests, and counseled others to do likewise.

At the time of Jesus, the Pharisees' predominant emphasis was on individual piety, but their obsession with the Law indirectly had social and political ramifications. The ordinary people looked up to them with respect and regarded them as their religious teachers and guides. The Pharisees were innovators in their belief that the basic biblical laws had to be expanded and interpreted to cover every detail of life. This was accomplished by oral interpretation; these decisions then had the force of law and affected the way people acted socially and politically. For instance, the Pharisees were conservative nationalists because they believed the way to preserve their faith was strict separation from the Gentiles and exact observance of the Law. Unlike the Sicarii and the Zealots, the Pharisees were not a social liberation movement that strove to elevate the depressed masses of Israel from hunger and poverty, but as it was required by the Law they did emphasize the giving of alms and generosity to the poor. Strict adherence to the Law then ultimately had social repercussions.

There is little evidence of Pharisaic political activity in relation to Rome during the life of Jesus (see Neusner). The Pharisees' principal concern was the Law, especially the rules for good observance and table fellowship that made it more difficult to associate with Romans and foreigners. However, when it came to conflicts over questions of the Law, they were ready to confront Rome in a nonviolent manner, even to the extent of risking their lives. For example, when Pilate became governor of Judea in A.D. 26, he came into Jerusalem by night with Roman soldiers carrying army standards bearing images of the Roman gods (Josephus, 18:3,1). This was prohibited by the first commandment of God. It was probably the Pharisees who placed their throats against the Roman soldiers' swords saying they would rather die than transgress the Law. Out of fear, Pilate was forced to remove the standards from Jerusalem.

The Sadduccees

The Sadduccees were religious conservatives and political moderates. They were conservative in that they held only the first five books of the Bible to be Torah or Law. They rejected the Pharisaic interpretations and decisions that would continually bring the law into new areas. For the Sadduccees, it was important to "return to fundamentals." They wanted reform through strict observance of only these basics. Consequently, they had more freedom in daily life and were better able to accommodate to Greek and Roman ways. The Sadduccees, many of whom were priests, were an elite group from the ruling class and richer families. Far from being social reformers, they were very much in favor of the status quo that supported their privileged position and power. They were wary of political and social revolutionaries, for if Rome fell their own power could be lost as well. They were moderates who hoped for a future temple-state that would centralize power about themselves with a minimum of Roman or foreign interference. Their attitude did change around A.D. 66 when they saw that the Temple and the religious institutions of Israel would be threatened if the Romans won another military victory over Israel.

The Essenes

This group is probably the same as the Dead Sea or Qumran community that attracted great attention when its scrolls were discovered in 1945. The Essenes lived a communitarian life in caves and buildings near the Dead Sea. They refused to have anything to do with the Jerusalem Temple. This was because the members felt that the temple priests had been unlawfully installed by the Maccabees after the struggle with Greece. They were like the Pharisees in their rigorous and exact interpretation of the Law. Applicants to the community had to prove themselves through a rigorous two-year novitiate before they could make their final oath to the group and commitment to its observances, at which time they were required to give all their property and possessions to the community. The group was very generous to the poor. In addition to the Law's requirements, the Essenes dedicated to the poor a day's income each month. Yet they were not a social movement in favor of the liberation of the poor and oppressed. From their documents we learn they had fervent hopes for the restoration of Israel through a priestly as well as kingly messiah. They looked forward to a final day of vengeance when God would win a great victory over the powers of evil. There is no record of political activity against Rome until the time of the Jewish War when they may have supported the struggle against Rome, believing that the empire represented the powers of evil. During the war, the Romans destroyed the Essenes' monastery and buildings.

John the Baptist's Movement

Around A.D. 30 an entirely new event was happening by the banks of the Jordan River. A fiery ascetic named John, who had long, uncut beard and hair, was proclaiming a radical message. He was announcing that the long expected Day of the Lord, the beginning of the kingdom of God, was close at hand. The great day of God's final intervention in the world was about to take place. John's message was brief but urgent: "Reform your lives! The reign of God is at hand" (Matt. 3:2).

John the Baptist asked all who heard him to confess their sins, sincerely promise to reform, and be baptized in the Jordan River. This last ritual was a surprising innovation. In Judaism only Gentile converts were required to be so baptized. Yet John said it was not enough to be circumcised or be a Jew. A new beginning, a complete conversion for everyone, was imperative. And he boldly said that a person's social class, political affiliations, and religious practices did not matter. Gender and race did not matter—the requirements were the same for all. Anyone who came to John at the Jordan was welcomed by him and invited to be baptized and forgiven (Matt. 21:32; Luke 3:12–14).

Of all the Palestine liberation movements of the time, the Baptist's movement was the most strict and demanding. With his insistence on a return to the core of the prophetic message of justice, John appeared like a prophet resurrected from an earlier age. His acceptance of all classes of society was socially radical. For the Baptist, there were no privileged classes in Israel. All were equal before God and in need of radical reform.

John's movement also had strong political connotations. The words "kingdom of God" had strong political overtones. For John, the kingdom of God was not a spiritual concept but a definite realm in which people obeyed God and practiced justice. King Herod was well aware of this and had John the Baptist imprisoned as a prelude to his death. While the Gospels attribute John's death to his prophetic teaching, Josephus, the Jewish historian, notes that the motivation was political (Josephus, 5:2). Herod perceived John the Baptist's preaching and popularity as a definite threat to his rule.

SUMMARY

All the liberation movements in first-century Palestine were religiously motivated, and all advocated some type of reform—each group placing varying emphasis upon social, political, and religious reforms. Although at times some groups tended ostensibly to isolationism or political noninvolvement, each group's worldview ultimately had political and social repercussions. The Sicarii and Zealots favored direct, military action to overthrow the government, the Sicarii adding a messianic motif. The Pharisees, while emphasizing exact obedience to the Law, promoted nonviolent resistance to Rome in matters of conflict with religious belief. The Qumran community, while concentrating on its communitarian life, expected a kingly (political) as well as priestly messiah. The Sadduccees, while politically moderate, did wish to lessen Roman control of Israel and its religious institutions and, around the Jewish War, more strongly opposed Rome. The Baptist movement, with its teaching on the imminent kingdom, was a threat to King Herod and brought a quick response from him. These roots of political revolution bore fruit during the Jewish war.

In the social area, the Sicarii and Zealots arose from class conflicts and attracted wide support among poor peasants. The Sadduccees had little social thrust in their teachings because they were part of the dominant ruling class. The Pharisees considered individual obedience to the Law as the best way to change society. The Essenes, though only indirectly concerned with social problems, gave a part of their monthly income to the poor. John the Baptist with his openness to all classes of people, especially the poor and "sinners," opened the way for a social revolution.

With varying emphases the Palestine liberation movements that arose around Jesus' time all intertwined religious, social, and political concerns. One reason for this was the historical and oppressive factors at work in first-century Palestine. Another reason was that the archetypal leadership figures for these movements were God and the great prophetic leaders, especially Moses, of the Old Testament—all of whom had been sensitive to the plight of the people of Israel and had acted in history to liberate that people from oppression. Against the backdrop of these movements we can more fully understand Jesus' leadership.

THE DIMENSIONS OF JESUS' LEADERSHIP

Using this sketch of liberation movements, some comparisons and contrasts to the religious, social, and political dimensions of

Jesus' approach and ministry can be made. First of all, like all these movements, Jesus' approach was profoundly religious. In this area he was most similar to the Baptist: Jesus was baptized by him, was then his collaborator, and drew his first disciples from among John's followers (John 1:35-42). Jesus preached the same radical message as John: "Repent for the kingdom of God is at hand." Along with John, Jesus demanded a complete new beginning in the conversion experience—requiring confession of sins and baptism.

Although Jesus shared the Pharisees' zeal for applying the Law to every aspect of daily life, his perception of the Law differed from that of the Pharisees and the other groups. He may originally have been a Pharisee himself, for he freely associated with them. However, when Jesus' disciples pluck grains of wheat on the Sabbath, the Pharisees are quick to call attention to this breach of the Law. Jesus' reply to them is: "The sabbath was made for man, not man for the sabbath" (Mark 2:27). In other words, unlike many of the Pharisees and members and leaders of other groups, Jesus emphasized human needs and the spirit of religion over the letter of religious law.

In social terms, Jesus' apostolate differed significantly from a number of the movements of his time. He placed great emphasis upon the social dimension of his ministry, and this contrasted with the Essenes' and Pharisees' emphasis upon individual piety. Jesus did not wait for "perfect" observers to come and join him or carefully screen out all applicants, as did the Essenes. He finally parted with John the Baptist, who waited at the Jordan River for converts to come to him. Instead, Jesus went out to the streets, fields, and places where the ordinary people lived and worked. He took the initiative to invite them to become disciples. It did not matter who they were—tax collectors, sinners, fisherfolk. Jesus accepted them as they were, assured them of God's forgiveness and invited them to repent. Unlike other religious teachers of the day, he accepted women as disciples. Mark notes the group of women at Calvary and even gives their names. They were women who had been followers of Jesus from the beginnings of his ministry in Galilee (15:41-42).

Jesus' preaching of the good news of the kingdom was especially directed to the poor. Like the Sicarii, he drew most of his followers from the oppressed population of Galilee. He confined his preaching to peasant audiences and within small towns. These were the very groups and places most oppressed by the Herods, Rome, and the rich Jewish ruling class and landowners. When John the Baptists, from prison, sent messengers to Jesus to ask if he was really the messiah, Jesus sent the answer: "The poor have the good news preached to them" (Matt. 11:5). Jesus' was a social apostolate.

Did Jesus actually aspire to be a political leader? When he spoke of a coming kingdom was he referring to heaven or a purely spiritual realm? His words to Pilate, "My kingdom does not belong to this world," seem to convey this meaning (John 18:36a). However, with Jesus' next words we discover that he is talking about *how* the kingdom will come about, which will not be through the ordinary human means of a military revolution. Jesus says, "If my kingdom were of this world, my subjects would be fighting to save me from being handed over to the Jews" (18:36b). In speaking about the coming kingdom, Jesus was primarily describing affairs *on earth*. He was concerned about an immediate future beginning with his ministry. Albert Nolan in *Jesus before Christianity* writes:

> The good news of the kingdom of God was news about a future state of affairs *on earth* when the poor would no longer be poor, the hungry would be satisfied, and the oppressed would no longer be miserable. To say "Thy kingdom come" is the same as saying "Thy will be done on *earth* as it is in heaven" [46].

The kingdom of God has definite earthy implications. It must be an actual realm where justice is practiced and where the poor and hungry are not only fed but share the abundant resources of this earth. To accomplish this, human leadership and cooperation is necessary. This of course has political consequences.

Did Jesus think that he would be a political king or messiah over a group of people on earth? If we look at Mark's Gospel, we find that Jesus is very secretive about his inner identity. The first time his disciples mention "discipleship" is at the confession of Peter. Jesus does not deny to Peter that he is the messiah but warns him to be silent and rebukes him for his incorrect views on what that title means (Mark 8:27–33). The secrecy motif disappears when Jesus' death draws near. In his trial before the Sanhedrin, Jesus replies to the high priest's question "Are you the Messiah, the Son of the Blessed One?" by stating without hesitation, "I am" (14:61). When Pilate questions him, "Are you the king of the Jews?", Jesus' answer is a little ambiguous: "You are the one who is saying it" (15:2). Similar answers are found in Matthew 27:11 and in Luke 23:3. The evangelists may be phrasing Jesus' answer in this way to show that Jesus' title is not the same as that of terrorist leaders whose first intention was to overthrow Rome. Jesus did not see himself as a purely political leader, but he did understand the significant political implications of his teachings and actions. There is no question that Roman authority put Jesus to death under the charge of being a king or messiah. The Romans placed a sentence above his head on the cross with the words: "The King of the Jews" (Mark 15:26).

As for Jesus' disciples, there are indications that until the end of his life they considered him the messiah who would bring about the restoration of the earthly kingdom to Israel. During the final journey to Jerusalem, two of Jesus' closest disciples, James and John, were thinking about the proximate organization of this kingdom and what authoritative roles they could play in it. They asked Jesus, "See to it that we sit, one at your right and the other at your left, when you come into your glory" (Mark 10:37). This blatant request is toned down by Matthew, who has their mother make it for them (21:21). Luke omits it. Luke does note that on Easter Sunday the two disciples walking to Emmaus say to the mysterious stranger (who is the risen Jesus), "We were hoping that he was the one who would set Israel free" (24:21). Even after the resurrection, the disciples continue to await the earthly kingdom. In the Acts of the Apostles, they ask the risen Jesus, "Lord, are you going to restore the rule to Israel now?" (1:16).

What impressions did ordinary people have about Jesus as an earthly messiah? There is evidence that Jesus' miracles did excite messianic expectations. His miracles duplicated some of the great marvels worked by God through Moses in liberating Israel. On the occasion of the multiplication of the loaves, John's Gospel records that Jesus had to flee because the crowds wanted to make him a king (6:15) (see Montefiore). The same idea appears to be behind the parallel story in Mark (6:34–46), where Jesus hastily dismisses the crowds and goes off to a mountain by himself. The people were acutely aware of the political implications of Jesus' ministry.

In summary, by comparing Jesus with the liberation movements of his time, a number of conclusions can be stated. To begin, there is no reason to hold that Jesus was only a religious or spiritual leader of an other-worldly kingdom. He was indeed a radical religious reformer. At the same time, his approach was that of a social revolutionary concerned with the deprived classes of Israel. Politically, he envisioned a definite realm in which his teachings would be put into practice and lived. This entailed changes in the ruling structures of Israel; it demanded new leadership. We can conclude by reaffirming that Jesus was a religious, social, and political messiah—a leader who expected his followers to imitate him and collaborate with him.

Chapter 3

Good News for the Poor and Oppressed

Jesus' call to his disciples was an invitation of love, a love that respected the freedom of each person. Yet the demands of discipleship were rigorous. This was not intended to make discipleship hard for people but to make it possible for them to fully share in Jesus' work and imitate his actions. The command "follow me" was repeated again and again to those who wished to be with him. "Follow me" did not mean passive listening but full collaboration. In Mark's Gospel there is nothing that Jesus does that his disciples cannot do also. It is a do-it-yourself Gospel: Jesus preaches the coming kingdom of God; his followers do so also. Jesus heals sicknesses and casts out devils; the twelve, once they share Jesus' faith, do so also. Mark notes that after Jesus prepared the twelve, "They went off preaching the need of repentance. They expelled many demons, anointed the sick with oil, and worked many cures" (6:12–13).

JESUS' TEACHING AND RADICAL PROPHETIC VIEWS

The Old Testament prophetic tradition is an essential element of Jesus' preaching on the meaning of discipleship. Jesus studied the Old Testament scriptures, especially those about the prophets who continually recalled people to the core of God's covenant with them. However, at Jesus' time, most people regarded the prophets as men from the distant past. So it was an exciting new

25

event when John the Baptist appeared by the Jordan River with the clothes and message of one of these prophets. He wore a garment of camel's hair with a leather belt around his waist—the distinctive garb of the great prophet Elijah (2 Kings 1:8). It was Elijah the prophet, like another Moses, who had revived the religion of Yahweh when Israel had almost completely adopted fertility cults as its religion. John the Baptist also called for a new start, the basis of which was confession of sins and baptism. His clarion call, "Repent," was the same as that of the great biblical prophets. Everyone knew what this meant: a return to the core of the covenant between God and God's people. Jesus joined the Baptist in proclaiming the same message, a message that Isaiah has God express to the people of Israel in these words:

> Wash yourselves clean! Put away your misdeeds from before my eyes; cease doing evil; learn to do good. Make justice your aim: redress the wronged, hear the orphan's plea, defend the widow [1:16].

Through Jeremiah, God had spoken in a similar manner:

> Only if you thoroughly reform your ways and your deeds; if each of you deals justly with his neighbor; if you no longer oppress the resident alien, the orphan, and the widow; if you no longer shed innocent blood in this place . . . will I remain with you in this place [7:5–7].

Why was justice to the poor and hungry the core of the prophetic message? It came from the prophets' deep sensitivity to the very nature of God and their deep conviction of God's absolute sovereignty. Again and again they repeated that it was necessary to *know* God. The first words of God to Isaiah, the greatest Old Testament prophet, are a complaint that the people of Israel does not *know* its God: "An ox knows its owner, and an ass, its master's manger; but Israel does not know, my people has not understood" (1:3).

To know God is to know a God of justice. It is only with this understanding that God can be worshiped authentically. Rafael Avila, in his book *Worship and Politics*, examines the connection between worship and justice. He writes,

The transition from a religion based on a sacrificial system to one based on personal faith—open to the knowledge of God whose fundamental demand is for justice—moved toward a progressive realization under the influence of the prophets of Israel [27].

Because they stressed the interconnection between worship and justice, the prophets and Jesus came into open conflict with institutionalized religion and its leaders. (In this context "institutionalized religion" means the attempt to mediate God's blessings independent of any commitment to justice for the poor and oppressed.) Amos the shepherd prophet (eighth century B.C.) was a striking example of a prophet who entered such a conflict, in the midst of which Amaziah the Bethel priest asked the king to expel Amos because his message directly condemned sanctuary worship divorced from the concerns of the oppressed poor. Through Amos, God's hatred for worship, prayer, and liturgical song that was unconnected with the plight of the needy was announced:

> I hate, I spurn your feasts, I take no pleasure in your solemnities . . . . Away with your noisy songs: I will not listen to the melodies of your harps. But if you would offer me holocausts, then let justice surge like water and goodness like an unfailing stream [5:21–24].

Jesus echoed this prophetic call for justice when he stated that justice and reconciliation must accompany worship:

> If you bring your gift to the altar and there remember your brother has anything against you, leave your gift at the altar, go first to be reconciled with your brother, and then come and offer your gift [Matt. 5:24].

Jesus also followed the prophetic tradition when he placed compassion for the hungry above all religious laws, even those regarding the Sabbath. He revealed that when the Pharisees confronted him about his disciples plucking grains of wheat on the Sabbath. At the end of his account of that incident Matthew has Jesus add a quotation from the prophet Hosea: "It is mercy I desire and not sacrifice" (12:7; see Hos. 6:6).

The prophets and Jesus could never separate spirituality from practical justice. To worship God with silence about matters of justice was not to worship God at all. Of all the prophets, Ezekiel gave the most attention to the Spirit and the inner dimensions of religion. At the same time, he could not separate spiritual life from a life devoted to justice. God spoke to Ezekiel with these words:

> If a man . . . oppresses no one, gives back the pledge received for a debt, commits no robbery; if he gives food to the hungry and clothes the naked; if he does not lend at interest nor exact usury; if he holds off from evildoing, judges fairly between a man and his opponent; if he lives by my statutes and is careful to observe my ordinances, that man is virtuous—he shall surely live, says the Lord God [Ezek. 18:7-9]

It is very significant that the prophets *never* appealed for charity or generosity from the rich: instead they demanded justice based on the consistent biblical teaching that the earth and its resources can never be merely private property. Land is a gift of God that is only *lent* to human beings, not for the benefit of a few but for all equally. The earth belongs to the God of all people, who wants it used with mutual accessibility for the benefit of all. Accordingly, in the book of Leviticus God says, "The land shall not be sold in perpetuity; for the land is mine and you are but aliens who have become my tenants" (25:23).

To ensure this was put into practice, the Leviticus laws mandated that no land could be sold permanently to anyone outside the family or clan, fifty years being the maximum that outsiders could possess the land. The fiftieth year was called a Jubilee Year, and during it all land had to return to its original owners:

> This fiftieth year you shall make sacred by proclaiming liberty in the land for all its inhabitants. It shall be a jubilee for you, when every one of you shall return to his own property, every one to his family estate [Lev. 25:10].

In *Sharing Possessions, Mandate and Symbol of Faith*, Luke Johnson notes that we can only understand Jesus' difficult sayings on riches in light of this prophetic view of the use of land. Jesus' teachings on money were based on traditional, radical, prophetic teaching on land, possessions, and justice for the poor. Consequently, the Gospels highlight the story of a rich man who wanted to be a disciple of Jesus. After he stated a number of commandments to the man, Jesus looked at him and said, "There is one thing more that you must do. Go and sell what you have and give to the poor; you will then have treasure in heaven. After that, come and follow me" (Mark 10:21). The evangelist then notes that the man went away sad, for he had many possessions. The event was the special occasion of an important teaching on discipleship: Jesus turned and said to his disciples, "How hard it is for the rich to enter the kingdom of God." The disciples wondered about this statement so Jesus repeated it for extra emphasis. He said, "My sons, how hard it is to enter the kingdom of God! It is easier for a camel to pass through a needle's eye than for a rich man to enter the kingdom of God" (15:25).

For Jesus, as well as the prophets, the way in which a person used money and possessions was an issue that demanded a clear choice between God and idolatry:

No man can serve two masters. He will either hate one and love the other or be attentive to one and despise the other. You cannot give yourself to God and money [Matt. 6:24-25].

Luke, in the Acts of the Apostles, gives special attention to the matter of property and possessions. Following in the tradition of the prophets' and Jesus' teachings about property, Luke writes of the early Jerusalem community that "those who believed shared all things in common; they would sell their property and goods, dividing everything on the basis of each one's need" (2:45).

THE KINGDOM OF GOD: GOOD NEWS FOR THE POOR AND OPPRESSED

Jesus' radical approach was based upon the old prophetic teachings on societal reform. Yet there was also an entirely new element he brought into his ministry. This was his proclamation in word and action that the kingdom of God was close at hand. The word *kingdom* is repeated over one hundred times in the Gospels. Jesus was preoccupied with this kingdom, which is the subject of his most common prayer, the Our Father, and is enunciated clearly in the words "thy kingdom come." Before Jesus, the prophets had looked to a distant future—a great Day of the Lord—when God would intervene in the world to establish justice and peace. For Jesus, however, that great future was immediate; it was beginning through his ministry.

The inner power of the kingdom was the presence of the fullness of the Spirit of God. This Spirit was expected to break down class distinctions and be available to young and old, men and women. Joel's prophecy had promised this:

> Then afterward I will pour out my spirit upon all mankind. Your sons and daughters shall prophesy, your old men shall dream dreams, your young men shall see visions. Even upon the servants and the handmaids, in those days, I will pour out my spirit [3:1–2].

This Spirit would effect full forgiveness and acceptance by God; it would bring reconciliation with God. In his great new covenant prophecy, Jeremiah had concluded by announcing, "All from least to greatest shall know me, says the Lord, for I will forgive their evildoing and remember their sin no more" (31:34). Ezekiel had expressed it in terms of a miraculous "heart transplant" effected by the Spirit:

> I will sprinkle clean water upon you to cleanse you from all your impurities, and from all your idols I will cleanse you. I will give you a new heart and place a new spirit within you, taking from your bodies your stony hearts and giving you natural hearts [36:25–26].

The coming of the kingdom of God was God's own work, not the product of human action. It was God's kingdom, and only God could bring it about. However, this God was a God of history who worked in and through people as chosen instruments. Jesus believed that the kingdom would not come from outer space but through the agency of himself and his disciples: through God's working in them. The kingdom would be experienced in and through people.

An essential mark of the kingdom is that it is *good news for the poor*. This was the message that Jesus sent to John the Baptist in response to his inquiry if Jesus was indeed the promised one. Jesus responded, "Go back and report to John what you have seen and heard. . . . The poor have the good news preached to them" (Matt. 11:4–5). Luke explains Jesus' goal in his description of Jesus' first sermon in Nazareth. Jesus chooses the following reading from the prophet Isaiah:

> The spirit of the Lord is upon me; therefore he has anointed me. He has sent me to bring glad tidings to the poor, to proclaim liberty to captives, recovery of sight to the blind and release to prisoners to announce a year of favor from the Lord [4:18–19; from Isa. 61:1–2].

This reveals that Luke believed that a fundamental aspect of Jesus' ministry was the jubilee announcement of liberation for the poor. Matthew's account of the Sermon on the Mount announces the same theme in the Beatitutdes with their special blessings for the poor, the hungry, and the oppressed (5:3–12).

Women were one of the oppressed groups in Israel in Jesus' time, and his proclamation-in-action of the kingdom took a revolutionary turn when he welcomed women disciples. This was a great innovation because no rabbi at that time accepted women as disciples. John the Baptist had baptized women who came to him at the Jordan River, but all those who remained at the Baptist's side were men. Only Luke explicitly mentions the women by name—who accompanied Jesus on his journeys. However, the information is found implicitly in Mark when he names the women at the foot of the cross and notes that they were Jesus' followers from the beginnings of his ministry in Galilee (15:40–41). While Luke's explicit references to women emphasize their hidden presence all the way through Jesus' ministry, Mark may have deliberately downplayed this prominence of women when it became an embarrassment in some sectors of the early church (see Munro).

Jesus' proclamation of the kingdom as good news for the poor was also clearly manifested in his attempts to break down social and religious barriers created as a result of the biblical laws regarding "cleanness and uncleanness." Women, as has been noted, were especially subject to ritual disqualifications because of the holiness and taboos associated with blood. However, Jesus allowed himself to be touched by a woman with a continuous flow of blood, despite the caveats that such a person's condition was contagious in causing uncleanness to others (Mark 5:28-29; Lev. 15:25-27). Because of such matters, men did not usually speak with women publicly. Yet John's Gospel notes that Jesus surprised his disciples by speaking with a strange woman in public (4:27).

Jesus also extended his ministry to the sick, many of whom were marginalized or segregated as "unclean." Mark writes "Whenever he put in an appearance, in villages, in towns, or at crossroads, they laid the sick in market places, and begged him to let them touch just the tassel of his cloak. All who touched him got well" (6:56). Jesus touched a leper who came to him for healing, despite the terrible fear of physical and ritual contagion that forced these unfortunate individuals to keep a long distance away from every human being (Mark 1:40-41). Jesus spent significant amounts of time with those who today we would consider mentally ill. Most people avoided the mentally ill, believing them to be unclean because an "unclean spirit" or devils were within them. Jesus' ministry of exorcism was an important part of his good news to the poor because it went directly to those most hopelessly in need. Mark notes that Jesus "went through their synagogues preaching the good news and expelling demons throughout the whole of Galilee" (1:39).

The greatest barrier in Jesus' world was that between Jew and Gentile. This was due in great measure to the restrictive Jewish laws about table fellowship. The situation was seriously aggravated by the rapacity and greed of the members of the Roman military who looked for spoils and personal gain at the expense of the Jews. Jesus, however, was willing to extend his ministry to even a Roman centurion by curing his servant (Matt. 8:5-13; Luke 7:1-10). It was in this matter of relationship to the hated Romans that Jesus' attitude is the most surprising. Roman troops

were accustomed to force civilians to carry Roman equipment
and heavy burdens along the roads they traveled. The Romans
must have received many a silent or vocal curse at the end of the
required mile, sometimes walked under a burning hot sun. Instead Jesus teaches, with a loving smile on his face, "Should anyone press you into service for one mile, go with him two miles"
(Matt. 5:41). This saying results from Jesus' unique view of the
solidarity of humanity. All people, no matter who they are, are
brothers and sisters, part of one human family. Most people give
special attention to personal, family, tribal, and national bonds,
but Jesus extended the view of neighbor to any person in need of
help, even an enemy.

Jesus' concern for the oppressed and outcast was not just
"task-oriented." It flowed from a deep compassion for those
who were suffering and in pain. This is in accord with the Wisdom
tradition in which the basic quality of a wise person is defined as a
"listening heart." Matthew's Gospel draws special attention to
this quality of Jesus. At the beginning of his public ministry,
Jesus mingles with sinners at the Jordan River; he undergoes baptism with them, and he continues to associate with and be open to
sinners throughout his ministry. In the Sermon on the Mount,
Jesus sums up his teaching with the Golden Rule, "Treat others
the way you would have them treat you: this sums up the law and
the prophets" (7:12).

Matthew is anxious to show that Jesus' miracles are motivated
by compassion and identification with the sick and the disabled.
The evangelist writes:

> As evening drew on, they brought him many who were pos-
> sessed. He expelled the spirits by a simple command and
> cured all who were afflicted, thereby fulfilling what had
> been said through Isaiah the prophet: "It was our infirmi-
> ties he bore, our sufferings he endured" [8:16].

In quoting Isaiah, Matthew has in mind the prophet's description
of a servant of the Lord who suffered as his people did and identified himself with their afflictions even as far as death (Isa.
52:13–53:12). Jesus' going out to teach and his appointment of
the twelve are also motivated by compassion for the multitudes:

"At the sight of the crowds, his heart was moved with pity. They were lying prostrate from exhaustion, like sheep without a shepherd" (9:36). The miracle of the loaves began because Jesus felt deep sympathy for the crowds who were without provisions, and were far from their homes: "My heart is moved with pity for the crowd. By now they have been with me three days, and have nothing to eat. I do not wish to send them away hungry, for fear they may collapse on the way" (15:32).

Matthew sums up the theme of Jesus' identification with the poor, the hungry, and the afflicted in a last judgment that concludes the prepassion part of the Gospel. Jesus' words in this scene constitute his last testament. Identification with the needy is considered so important that it is described as a direct service to God (see Grassi 1981), done in obedience to Jesus' commands:

I was hungry, and you gave me food, I was thirsty and you gave me drink. I was a stranger and you welcomed me, naked and you clothed me. I was ill and you comforted me, in prison and you came to visit me [25:35-36].

For Luke this whole matter of identification and sensitivity is so important that the command, "love your neighbor" has no meaning without it. In the Good Samaritan parable, only deep pity moves the foreigner who goes to the aid of an unknown Jew lying beside the road: "A Samaritan who was journeying along came on him and was moved to pity at the sight" (10:34). This Greek text has the word *esplangnistheis*—literally that his "insides were stirred." The Good Samaritan's action prompts a redefinition of the fallen Jew's neighbor: The new definition is "The one who treated him with compassion" (10:37). The only lesson from the story is the simple concluding words of Jesus: "Go and do the same" (10:37).

SUMMARY

The message of John the Baptist and Jesus—repent—was a renewal of the ancient prophetic tradition. These prophets had a keen insight into God's nature as a God of justice for the poor and oppressed. The prophets condemned as false worship or idolatry all worship that did not include justice for the poor. This included the realization that all land was a gift from God and could never be used for the advantage of a few persons. Jesus returned to the prophetic core of the covenant in his rigorous requirements for discipleship.

Jesus' ministry, however, took an entirely new direction. He lived and acted in view of an imminent coming of the kingdom of God. The special feature of this kingdom was a program of good news for the poor. Jesus put this in practice through a revolution in the meaning of service. Energy and time were not only to be used for obtaining life's necessities; they were unique opportunities and gifts, given to be used in loving and personal service to the underprivileged. This service drew its inspiration not from a sense of duty or law but from a deep feeling of compassion and identification with those in need.

Chapter 4

The Kingdom of God and the Kingdom of Satan: The Temptation of Power

JESUS' HOLY WAR AGAINST SATAN'S KINGDOM

The last chapter focused on Jesus' proclamation in words and action of good news for the poor and oppressed. However, this is not the only force at work in the Gospels: on almost every page we find a struggle against the forces of evil. In Jesus' society, the forces of evil were embodied in the rich Jewish ruling classes and were supported by Roman power and greed. Jesus was engaged in a holy war against the kingdom of Satan that held sway in this world.

This kingdom of Satan drew its support from selfishness, greed, and human desires for pleasure and personal gain. Satan drew many followers from those aspiring to prestige, money, power, and control over others. In Jesus' society prestige was the most important value; it was more important than money. This prestige was based on many factors: ancestry, authority, education, wealth, and "virtue." It affected every facet of life: how a person addressed others and how that person was greeted in return: who invited one to social functions and whom one invited in return; where one sat in the synagogue or at a banquet (Nolan, 54). Jesus directly opposed this kingdom of Satan both by action and word. He combatted selfishness through service to the needy and sick. He made prestige seem ridiculous by his attention to children and those—such as tax collectors, sinners, and the mentally ill—carefully avoided by religious leaders. Jesus also took a public and determined stand against those who oppressed the ordinary people. He maintained these convictions even though his stand resulted in fierce opposition and finally led to his arrest and death.

The Gospels single out Jesus' cleansing of the Temple as a full confrontation with the upper-class priests controlling the Temple. These priests were also part of the rich ruling class of Israel. These men were not content with the usual support due to them from every offering made in the Temple. They also made substantial profits on all business and market transactions carried out in the outer court of the Temple. In the Old Testament the prophet Zechariah had written about a last day when God would purify the holy Temple (14:20-21). The popular interpretation of this text was that God would purify the Temple of hated foreigners and Gentiles (see Roth). This interpretation was based on the last words of Zechariah, ''There shall be no longer any merchant [literally 'Canaanite'] in the house of the Lord of hosts'' (14:21). The word *Canaanite* was usually translated as ''foreigner'' because the Israelites had driven the Canaanites out of the land of promise. However, the word could also be translated in its original sense of ''trader'' or ''businessman.'' This is the way that Jesus understood the text, and he put this interpretation into action through a symbolic cleansing of the Temple in a way that recalled Zechariah:

> He entered the temple precincts and began to drive out those who were engaged in buying and selling. He overturned the moneychangers' tables and the stalls of the men selling doves; moreover, he would not permit anyone to carry things through the temple area [Mark 11:15-16].

Jesus intended to restore the Temple to its original purpose as a house of prayer. Instead of closing it to Gentiles, he wanted to open it to the world. Jesus' action was dangerous both to himself and to his disciples. The response to it marked the beginning of a determined course of action by his opponents that would soon lead to his death. The chief priests and ruling class were well aware of its meaning as a direct threat to their position and authority. Mark tells us that the chief priests and scribes heard of what he did and began to look for a way to destroy him (11:18).

Jesus' open preaching about the kingdom was also a direct threat to Rome. The kingdom, even if it came from God and not from military force, meant a new social order and structural change. This was a direct challenge to Roman authority. Herod had already destroyed John the Baptist because he considered him politically dangerous. Rome would take very seriously any popular movement intent on social change.

The first three Gospels give special attention to Jesus' reply when asked if it was lawful to pay tribute to the Roman emperor. At first glance, Jesus' answer seems to reflect a concern for order, taxes, and authority: "Give to Caesar what is Caesar's but give to God what is God's" (Mark 12:17). However, the stress is on the second part of the statement: "*but* give to God what is God's." This implies the total service to God that is enunciated in the first and second commandments. It acknowledges absolute dominion of God. As we have seen, the Old Testament prophets who taught about God's sovereignty made no compromises. Worship of God meant a commitment to God's justice. It was also a matter of loving God "with all your heart, and with all your soul, and with all your strength" (Deut. 6:5). Any debt to Caesar should be viewed in relation to this total service to God. So Jesus' reply was actually an implied threat to Rome. In Luke's Gospel, Jesus' enemies interpret his answer in just such a way. In Jesus' trial before Pilate they say, "We found this man subverting our nation, opposing the payment of taxes to Caesar, and calling himself the Messiah, a king" (23:2–3).

THE TEMPTATION OF POWER

In chapter 2 we saw that many people, including Jesus' disciples, thought he would be the leader over an earthly kingdom. The Old Testament repeatedly expressed the idea that a leader or king is expected to use his power to establish justice. Isaiah had written that the messianic king would "judge the poor with justice and decide aright for the land's afflicted '' (11:4). Psalm 72 is a prayer that the king might use God's power to establish justice in the land:

> O God, with your judgment endow the king,
>   and with your justice, the king's son;
> He shall govern your people with justice
>   and your afflicted ones with judgment.
> The mountains shall yield peace for the people,
>   and the hills justice.
> He shall defend the afflicted among the people,
>   save the children of the poor,
>   and crush the oppressor [72:1-4].

In view of these texts we can understand the common expectation that a king would use earthly power to establish justice for the poor and the oppressed. There is reason to believe, however, that Jesus regarded the use of dominative power—the power that subjugates and controls people and things—as a serious danger to his mission. The tenor of his whole preaching was that only God would bring about the kingdom; no strictly human power could. There are indications that Jesus looked upon the possibility of using dominative power, even to accomplish good, as the most serious temptation of his life.

The Gospels see this temptation following Jesus from the beginning of his career until his arrest and death. It has become almost commonplace to describe the temptation as Jesus' refusal to become a temporal messiah and his choice instead to be a teacher or religious messiah. However, this type of statement has far-reaching consequences. It brings Jesus and Christians to a nonpolitical stance, reducing the Gospel to a matter of individual piety. We have already seen that there is no evidence for the view that the messiah was a purely spiritual leader. The question Jesus faced was not whether he would become a spiritual or a temporal leader. It concerned the *means* by which he and his followers would establish a new societal order based on justice. Could this means be dominative power, force, and violence?

Both Matthew and Luke have Jesus' temptation immediately following his baptism. The first temptation is to change stones into bread to relieve his own hunger and that of others. Jesus replies with the words of Deuteronomy 8:3, "Not by bread alone does man live, but by every word that comes forth from the mouth of God" (Matt. 4:4). To perform miraculous works of power is not Jesus' way: instead his way is obedience to God as the source of all nourishment. This implies that if the hungry are to be fed, the followers of Jesus must be brought to the same obedience to a God of justice. The second temptation is for Jesus to throw himself from the temple parapet and float to the ground in a great display of power. This would virtually force people to believe in him. Jesus answers, "You shall not put the Lord your God to the test" (Matt. 4:7). This "test" would be whether God, at Jesus' insistence, would perform works of power; it would lessen the importance of inner obedience to God's commands and word. The third temptation presents Jesus with a vision of his being king over the entire world. In asking for homage, the devil is asking Jesus to follow other plans instead of those of God. The devil lays before Jesus the way of the kingdom of Satan, which relies on force and power—the only effective way known to the devil. Jesus replies, "You shall do homage to the Lord your God; him alone shall you adore" (Matt. 4:10). Jesus' way is based on the first commandment: recognition of the absolute sovereignty of God and the necessity to follow God's will. The kingdom can only come through God's power, not through any human reliance on dominative power or force.

Another great crisis takes place during the multiplication of the loaves. As already noted, at this time in Jesus' ministry the people (and probably the disciples) are enthusiastic about making Jesus a king. Jesus is profoundly disturbed, for he knows that any such action will have to be based on political and perhaps military force. Jesus is forced to dismiss the crowd and the disciples. Faced with the enticing temptation of power—a quick and very tangible human way to get things done—Jesus goes off to pray for strength (John 6:14–15).

Still another hour of crisis comes during Jesus' prayer in the Garden of Olives, just before his arrest. It is the time of the final great crisis in Jesus' life. He knows Judas has been plotting his arrest and is perhaps already on the way with soldiers to capture him. At this moment Jesus has two possiblities open to him. He can perservere in his plan to stay in Jerusalem to be faithful as a prophet in announcing the good news of the kingdom—but this will mean certain death. Or, he can escape. He can leave Jerusalem under the cover of night and retire into Galilee where he can gather more followers, thus strengthening his position. Yet if he follows the second alternative, he will not be trusting his Father's will that he be faithful to his prophetic call in the very region where his message is most needed. If he chooses the first alternative, death could bring an early end to his ministry, which is so necessary for the coming of the kingdom. The dilemma seems impossible to resolve. Overcome by fear and uncertainty, Jesus falls to the ground and asks for strength to do his Father's will. Again and again he prays, "Thy will be done." Finally, after hours of agonizing struggle, Jesus decides not only to await his arrest but even to go out to meet Judas and his cohorts (Mark 14:32–52). Jesus trusts in what seems absolutely impossible from a human point of view: God's power to establish the kingdom even in the face of suffering and death. He resists the temptation to escape and use human means and force to become the chosen leader of his people.

The Gospels present the temptation of power as continuing even to the moment of Jesus' death on the cross. Those who pass by the crucifixion jeer at Jesus and mock him saying, "Save yourself now by coming down from that cross." Even the chief priests and scribes join the mockery by saying, "He saved others but he cannot save himself! Let the 'Messiah,' the 'king of Israel,' come down from that cross here and now so that we can see it and believe in him!" (Mark 15:31–32). Again Jesus resists the temptation to control people and things.

Was Jesus then in favor of "nonresistance"? Did he advocate not only refraining from violence but also avoiding actions and words that confront those responsible for evil? Not by any means! Jesus, even at the risk of his life, directly confronted those who were the cause of injustice. We noted this in the cleansing of the Temple, which appears to be the immediate cause of the plot leading to his death.

Was Jesus then a pacifist? Did he believe that violence resulting in death or injury to others is never permitted? The Bible does not condemn the armed liberation struggles—from that of David against the Philistines to that of the Maccabees against Greek domination—that are mentioned or depicted within it. In fact, such struggles are even praised and supported in the Bible. Jesus himself never condemned the armed underground guerilla movements of groups like the Zealots. There are statements in the Sermon on the Mount about "turning the other cheek" and not offering resistance to the evil doer. However, these statements are directions put together by Matthew for Christians who were undergoing persecution for their faith. Jesus was not strictly a pacifist.

He was a pacifist *and* an activist. He was convinced that the kingdom of God, with its dimensions of justice and peace, could not be accomplished by dominative power, force, and violence. The kingdom had to come from God. Jesus was convinced that God's kingdom had to be demonstrated in action through a ministry of good news for the oppressed, the poor, and the sick. People needed revolutionary inner conversion in order to turn from pursuits of selfishness, pleasure, money, and prestige to loving service to others, especially the poor. This would be accompanied by a return to the basic prophetic teaching that no true worship of God could take place unless it was accompanied by justice.

The rejection of the temptation to use dominative power is an important theme of the gospel message. However, the kingdom of God is a visible human realm, and in that realm power is a reality. Jesus, then, does not reject all uses of power. His words and actions say that earthly power, by itself, cannot bring about the kingdom of God; in order to promote that kingdom people first must have a revolutionary inner conversion that links them in obedience to God, who is a God of justice. That conversion in the inner core of individuals will then necessitate service to the poor and oppressed, the promotion of justice, and, ultimately, drastic social changes that involve the use of property and the earth's resources for all. Thus, Jesus rejected the use of domination to bring about the ideal society but never absolutely condemned all forms of power. He did not condemn the inner power that ultimately leads a person to confront and resist the forces of oppression and injustice. His attitude was that in the struggle for true justice and peace in human society we must strive to use a minimum of force and a maximum of the inner resources of the kingdom.

Chapter 5

The Inner Resources of the Kingdom: Faith, Prayer, the Spirit

THE INNER POWER OF FAITH AND PRAYER

For Jesus as a Jew, Abraham was the great example of an extraordinary quality called faith. One night God took Abraham outside to gaze at the brilliant sky of the ancient Middle East. God said to him, "Look up at the sky and count the stars, if you can. Just so shall your descendants be" (Gen. 15:5). Abraham was simply bewildered at this promise because, at the time, he had no heir. Later, after Abraham was circumcised, God became more specific: Abraham was told he would have a child by Sarah, his wife, and that they would become the parents of a multitude of nations. This was too much for even the faithful Abraham. He fell prostrate on the ground and could not resist laughing. He said, "Can a child be born to a man who is a hundred years old? Or can Sarah give birth at ninety?" (Gen. 17:17).

What God told Abraham sounded ridiculous, yet the word *faith* is actually derived from the Latin *ridere,* to laugh. Despite his hesitation and laughter, Abraham did believe, and a child was born to the aged couple. The child, Isaac, was the father of Jacob, the progenitor of the twelve tribes of Israel. When Abraham's child was born, Sarah could think of no better name to call him than Isaac, which means "laughter." She said, "God has given

43

me cause to laugh, and all who hear of it will laugh with me"
(Gen. 21:6).

The core of biblical faith is that "nothing shall be impossible
with God." This was the faith that moved Jesus to face impossible situations with hope and confidence. This faith reflected a
deep interior openness and surrender to God. In Jesus' case this
obedient surrender was to the truth of the message that God had
entrusted to him: the coming kingdom of God. This faith was also
the basic quality that Jesus asked of his disciples. The Gospels
emphasize that Jesus required this faith of all those people who
came to him for cures. Faith was the interior healing and conversion that made the outward cure possible. Jesus claimed no magi-
cal power for healing others. He told his disciples they could
duplicate what he did if they had the same faith.

Mark illustrates this kind of faith through the story of the healing of the epileptic boy in chapter nine of his Gospel. The boy was
in a hopeless state when his father brought him to Jesus' disciples
for a cure. Jesus had gone to a high mountain for the transfigura-
tion. Although the disciples tried to help, they were not able to
heal the afflicted boy. Upon Jesus' return, the father brought his
son to him, reasoning that the master had superior powers. The
father said to Jesus, "If out of the kindness of your heart you can
do anything to help us, please do!" (9:22). Behind these words
was the father's feeling that performing the miracle was only a
question of whether Jesus was willing to use his special powers to
cure the boy. Jesus understood this and gave the unusual answer,
" 'If you can'? Everything is possible to a man who trusts." In
other words, the problem was not with Jesus' willingness but
within the man himself: If *you* can (believe). The father finally
realized this and replied, "I do believe! Help my lack of trust."
After evoking this prerequisite of faith, Jesus went ahead and
cured what was considered an incurable illness. The real lesson of
the story was directed at Jesus' disciples (and every believer).
They came privately to him afterward and asked why they had
failed. Jesus replied, "This kind you can drive out only by
prayer." Only prayer and deep faith were lacking on their part,
nothing else.

Faith and prayer are closely intertwined. Faith is the interior disposition of openness to God in face of the impossible. Prayer is the outward activation of this faith through the whole body in words and gestures. The essential quality of prayer is absolute confidence, even in the face of impossible obstacles. Mark has Jesus teach this immediately after the decisive action of the cleansing of the Temple—an action that prompted Jesus' enemies to plan his capture and death. How can official Jerusalem, a "mountain" of opposition, be overcome? Jesus said to the disciples:

> Put your trust in God. I solemnly assure you, whoever says to this mountain, 'Be lifted up and thrown into the sea,' and has no inner doubts but believes that what he says will happen, shall have it done for him. I give you my word, if you are ready to believe that you will receive whatever you ask for in prayer it shall be done for you [Mark 11:23-24].

Within these unusual words we find Jesus' secret of prayer: to have such confidence in it that before one begins praying, the desired objective of the prayer is already believed a reality. This image, bred in confidence, is part of the prayer itself, adding special energy to effect the outcome. This trust is based on Jesus' view of God as having greater love and concern for God's children than any human parent. So Jesus said in the Sermon on the Mount: "If you, with all your sins, know how to give your children what is good, how much more will your heavenly Father give good things to anyone who asks him" (Matt. 7:11).

Speaking in his native Aramaic tongue, Jesus himself expressed this confidence by addressing God with the word *abba* (Mark 14:36). This was used of human fathers and still is used in that sense in modern Israel. It was never used in Jesus' time to speak directly to God. The more formal Hebrew *our father* was used. *Abba* was a term reserved for intimate family circles. This word had precious memories for early Christians. They liked to pray using the exact unusual address to God that Jesus himself had used—despite the fact that non-Jewish Christians did not know Aramaic but spoke Greek and other languages (Gal. 4:6; Rom. 8:15). In chapter 8 it will be shown that *abba* has a very special sense, that of a dedicated, obedient child addressing his or her father. Thus this word underscores the meaning of faith as obedience and surrender to God (see Grassi 1982).

Prayer was of especial importance to Jesus in the long periods when he retired from the disciples and crowds—during the great crises of his ministry. After his baptism Jesus had to make important decisions about the type of leader he would be for his people. To be able to do this, he fasted forty days and forty nights. After the multiplication of loaves, the enthusiastic crowds attempted to force Jesus into the role of a military messiah (John 6:46). Jesus had to dismiss the crowds and go off to a mountain to pray. Before his arrest Jesus prayed for hours in the Garden of Olives. He needed prayerful strength to make the decision to enter into events that would surely lead to his death.

Prayer was also an essential part of Jesus' daily life. He faced each event with a deep trust in his mission and in the powers of the Spirit. In his depiction of a typical day during Jesus' ministry, Mark describes Jesus as rising early before daybreak to go off by himself and pray (1:35–39). During the day Jesus' form of prayer was in the Jewish tradition of the mantra or frequently repeated short prayer. We find this tradition described in the central daily Jewish prayer, called the Shemah or Hear O Israel, with its familiar words: "The Lord is our God, the Lord alone. Therefore you shall love the Lord, your God, with all your heart, and with all your soul, and with all your strength" (Deut. 6:4). The instructions following the prayer indicate it should be repeated at home, while traveling, while busy at work, and while at rest (6:7).

The Lord's Prayer is not a formula for prayer but a series of mantras or short petitions that were used again and again by Jesus, from whom the disciples learned to pray. The short expressions "thy kingdom come" or "thy will be done" were of this nature. Both Matthew and Mark describe Jesus' prayer on the Mount of Olives as consisting of petitions of the Our Father. In Matthew the words "thy will be done" and "lead us not into temptation" from the Lord's Prayer are found almost word for word in Jesus' prayer in the garden (26:41, 43). For Jesus prayer was not an occasional exercise but an important element of each day and each hour of the day.

THE SPIRIT AND BREATH OF GOD

Faith and prayer are inner resources that are prerequisites for the coming of the kingdom of God. Yet these two elements might be called the "subjective" side of these resources—the human dispositions necessary for the "objective" divine power to work. For Jesus and his disciples this divine power did not come from a distant God who only came near in times of crisis. God was addressed as "father in heaven" but this was only to affirm that God was completely beyond and above all of creation and not to be identified with the sun, moon, stars, or anything in the universe. Within the world, God's presence was in all things, sustaining all life, and guiding the events of history. This presence was called the Spirit.

The word *spirit* comes from a translation of the Hebrew *ruach,* which is closely associated with breath, air, and wind. The Hebrews believed the universe was filled with divine energy that was the source of all life, activity, and movement. This divine energy was especially evident in the breathing of animals, human beings, and the earth itself, the movements of air being the earth's breath. The breathing of humans began at birth in a mysterious way and was beyond human control. It ended just as mysteriously at death. It was indeed an unexplainable gift. Thus a life-spirit came into human beings at birth and returned to its source at death.

In line with this view, the creation of man and woman in the Bible is described as a sharing of God's own life-energy; God breathes Spirit into them: "The Lord God formed man out of the clay of the ground and blew into his nostrils the breath of life, and so man became a living being" (Gen. 2:7). Through this story the biblical author teaches that there is a mysterious divine element within each human being resulting from a direct connection with the source of all life. This inner presence of the breath/spirit of God is so important that it is the most precious human possession. In the book of Job, the author proudly proclaims: "The breath of God is in my nostrils" (27:3). When biblical authors wished to say "every living thing," they wrote "all in whose nostrils is the breath of life" (Gen. 7:22).

However, the biblical writers realized that the gift of the Spirit of God in human life was only part of the great Spirit that fills the universe. The book of Wisdom proclaims that the "Spirit of the Lord fills the world" (1:7). As the writers looked to the future, they predicted a coming Day of the Lord when the fullness of God's Spirit would pour upon the earth. The prophet Joel described this as a universal outpouring of the Spirit in the last days of history (3:1–2). Ezekiel, at the time of the Exile, spoke of this coming Spirit in terms of a "heart transplant" that would give a new interior dimension to each person (36:26). The prophet Isaiah taught that in this coming new age a great leader, with a special infusion of the Spirit, would lead God's kingdom. He described this future son of David in these terms:

> The Spirit of the Lord shall rest upon him: a spirit of wisdom and of understanding, a spirit of counsel and of strength, a spirit of knowledge and of fear of the Lord [11:2].

With this biblical background we can appreciate the tremendous impact that the descent of the Holy Spirit had upon Jesus at the beginning of his ministry. It gave a special new orientation to his entire life and activity. Mark describes this as a vision that Jesus alone had, a personal, inner vision that was a secret to Jesus himself:

> Immediately on coming up out of the water, he saw the sky rent in two and the Spirit descending on him like a dove. Then a voice came from the heavens: "You are my beloved Son. On you my favor rests" [1:10–11].

From what follows in the Gospels, this descent of the Spirit appears to be a special messianic designation of Jesus that impels him to begin his public ministry. The Spirit also gave him the guidance and energy necessary to accomplish it. This was the deep interior and personal element that was Jesus' most important inner resource.

The text notes that the Spirit came upon him "like a dove." The dove's image had special meaning for every Jew. It was particularly associated with love, intimate friendship, and marriage. The phrase *my dove* was a favorite expression used in courtship and marriage. It is found several times in the great love poem of the Bible, the Song of Songs. The lover speaks intimately to his spouse and refers to her as a dove: "Open to me my sister, my beloved, my perfect one" (5:2); "one alone is my dove, my perfect one" (6:9). The image of the dove is drawn from everyday life in which people observed that doves were gentle and peaceful, staying close to one another in pairs for long periods of time.

For Jesus the dove's image had a deep, interior, and personal meaning. It was the symbol of an inner marriage with the Spirit that would give him loving energy and support in the difficult times that lay ahead. His baptism taught him to rely on the inner presence of the Spirit to bring about the kingdom, no matter what the obstacles might be. Two verses after his description of Jesus' baptism, Mark notes that John the Baptist had been arrested. In those days this was a usual prelude of death. As an associate of the Baptist, Jesus would also be in danger. Yet despite this, he decided to begin his ministry, following in the footsteps of the Baptist. In the Gospels, Jesus' baptismal experience is a model for disciples and early Christians. John the Baptist proclaimed that Jesus in turn would be the one who "baptizes with the Holy Spirit" (Mark 1:8; Matt. 3:11; Luke 3:16). Jesus would be the one who would renew for people the intimate, interior experience of a dovelike Spirit, an experience that would be an inner resource and wellspring of strength in times of hardship and suffering.

More than the other evangelists, Luke in his Gospel develops the intimate relationship between Jesus and the Spirit as a model for Christians. Only Luke mentions Jesus' praying after his baptism and before the descent of the Spirit. The evangelist suggests that in this scene Jesus is praying for the coming of the Spirit; Luke gives greater emphasis to the Spirit than to the baptism (3:21–22). Luke's version of the Lord's Prayer, according to some Greek manuscripts, has the petition, "May your Holy Spirit come" (11:2). In the prayer instruction that follows, Luke's version has Jesus saying "how much more will the heavenly Father give the *Holy Spirit* to those who ask him" (11:13). In contrast, the parallel text in Matthew has "*good things* to those who ask him'' (7:11). Luke highlights the special guidance and direction of the Holy Spirit in the ministry of Jesus: Jesus is led out of temptation in the desert by the Spirit (4:1); he returns to Galilee in the power of the Spirit (4:14); for his first sermon in Nazareth he chooses the Isaian text "the spirit of the Lord is upon me" (4:18); when he prays, he "rejoiced in the Holy Spirit" (10:21).

Luke has all this in his Gospel as a prelude to his second volume, the Acts of the Apostles, in which he carefully indicates that the same Spirit that guided Jesus also guides the early church. Just as Jesus prayed for the Spirit's coming, so the early Christians assemble at Pentecost and pray for the Spirit to come. As a result, they experience the breath of the Spirit as a mighty wind moving through the house and as visibly apparent in the tongues of fire and the ecstatic speech of the disciples. With this new power they have courage, like Jesus, to begin their ministry to the world (2:1–4). Just as the Spirit guided Jesus' ministry, so the same Spirit directs those who extend Jesus' mission to the world. Stephen, one of the early Greek Christian leaders, is described as a man full of the Holy Spirit (6:8; 7:55). This is the same description Luke in his Gospel has given to Jesus (4:1). The Holy Spirit takes the initiative in selecting Paul for a special mission to the Gentiles (13:3). When Paul and Barnabas depart, they are described as "sent by the Holy Spirit" (13:4).

Thus Jesus' obedience to God and his reliance upon the inner resources of faith, prayer, and the Spirit serve as a model for the disciples, for the early church, and for all followers of Jesus. Jesus' radical obedience to God leads to his death. That death, that sacrifice, and its eucharistic memorial can be understood fully only when viewed in relationship to Jesus' use of the inner resources (see chap. 8). Jesus demands that his disciples develop these resources, this openness and obedience to God and the Spirit. Those inner powers must be cultivated if the poor and hungry are to be liberated. Jesus showed that through these interior wellsprings and absolute confidence in God even overwhelming obstacles can be overcome. Faith, prayer, and the Spirit have greater strength than the dominative power used to oppress and starve people. Jesus showed that by following his commands to feed the hungry and by using these inner powers, a miracle of sharing can be produced that will result in the hungry being fed.

Chapter 6

Food and Discipleship

OLD TESTAMENT BACKGROUND

There is a strong gospel tradition that sharing food with the hungry was one of Jesus' special concerns. The miracle of the loaves occupies a central place in all the Gospels. In Matthew, Mark, and Luke it is the climax of the series of Jesus' miracles and comes just before the confession of Peter. In John it marks a turning point and crisis in Jesus's life. In all the Gospels it is meant to parallel the greatest epiphanies of God in the Old Testament: the miraculous manna appearing in the desert and the crossing of the Red Sea.

It is God who provides manna in the desert for a hungry people. During their stay on the barren Sinai Peninsula, the Israelites depleted their food supplies and were unable to obtain or buy more provisions. The people cried out to Moses and God for help. God answered and promised them flesh to eat in the evening and "in the morning your fill of bread." When the people rose in the morning, they found "fine flakes like hoarfrost on the ground" (Exod. 16:15). They exclaimed in Hebrew, "Man hu?", which means "what is this?" and from which the word *manna* derives. Moses answered, "This is the bread which the *Lord* has given you to eat" (16:15).

There is another and very important part of this story. The whole community obtained sufficient food only because a second "miracle" of sharing took place. In the story every able-bodied person went out to gather the miraculous bread. Some were able

51

to gather large amounts, others very little. Yet God commanded that at the end of the day all should share equally, regardless of the amount they gathered. In this way all the people, the old, the sick, the handicapped, had enough. The Israelites followed God's command, and the Bible notes that when they measured out the bread, "he who had gathered a large amount did not have too much, and he who had gathered a small amount did not have too little. They so gathered that everyone had enough to eat" (Exod. 16:18).

JESUS' COMMAND TO FEED THE HUNGRY

The New Testament story of the multiplication of loaves, in striking parallel to the Exodus story, still retains the primary elements of a miraculous sharing of food. Like the Israelites, the crowds in the gospel story are in a desperate situation. They are in a desert place far from their homes and any supply of food. Matthew, Mark and Luke draw special attention to Jesus' command to his disciples: "You yourselves give them to eat" (Matt. 14:16; Mark 6:37; Luke 9:13). This command is found word for word in these three Gospels, although Luke reverses the order of words. The addition (though not needed) of the Greek second person pronoun adds special emphasis to the command given the disciples: *you yourselves* are the ones who should provide the food.

All the Gospels record the disciples' sense of frustration at these words. In Mark's Gospel, Jesus adds, "How many loaves do you have? Go and see" (8:18). These words seem to imply that the disciples should find out whether any people have bread to share. They find only a few loaves—five or seven in the various stories—and this seems a ridiculously small amount for a huge crowd. John's Gospel highlights this by including the incident of a child who comes up to the disciples with a few loaves of bread and dried fish he had been saving (6:9). Just as in the Sinai episode, it is this miracle of sharing that makes it possible for Jesus to begin the distribution of the loaves. In other words, a miracle of sharing lies at the heart of the loaves miracle. The sharing of the fish and loaves, begun by the child and then continued by the disciples, is an obedient response to Jesus' command, "You yourselves give them to eat."

If we look into the Old Testament background, we will find more indications of the importance of Jesus' command as a prophetic announcement that embodies all the power of God (see Grassi 1978). The miracle of the loaves in the Gospels forms a literary parallel to a similar loaves miracle by the prophet Elisha:

A man came from Baal-shalishah bringing the man of God twenty barley loaves made from the first fruits, and fresh grain in the ear. "Give it to the people to eat," Elisha said. But his servant objected, "How can I set this before a hundred men?" Elisha insisted, "For thus says the Lord, 'They shall eat and there shall be some left over.' " And when they had eaten, there was some left over, as the Lord had said [2 Kings 4:42–44].

The striking parallels of Jesus' multiplication of the loaves to Elisha's miracle make it likely that the evangelists are emphasizing Jesus' words as a prophetic command with all the power of the word of God. A few of these parallels are: the order to give the people food; the objections about the impossible command; the emphasis on the remaining superabundant bread.

Although Mark does not develop and explain the application of this prophetic command of Jesus to feed the hungry, it must be remembered that his Gospel was written for church instruction, and his readers and listeners would have regarded Jesus' command as permanent and written for them. They would have understood that they were to imitate Jesus' example. Matthew's Gospel is more explicit and has a central theme built around Jesus' commands, especially to feed the hungry. Jesus' words "I was hungry and you gave me to eat" constitute a climax of Jesus' teaching in a great judgment scene just before the passion account. This is by no means accidental. All of Matthew's Gospel is meant to be a new Torah; it is intended to be a guide to a way of life based on Jesus' instructions and commands. In the concluding verses of Matthew, the twelve are sent to the entire world as teachers. They are to pass on Jesus' commands and instructions and see to it that they are obeyed: "Teach them to carry out everything that I have commanded you."

Matthew also emphasizes Jesus' instructions to his followers to identify with him (see Grassi 1981): "As long as you did it to one of my least brothers, you did it to me" (25:40). This identification motif can be better understood in terms of its Old Testament background. God's commandments were not understood in an impersonal or legalistic sense. Keeping them was considered a personal service to God. So commandments and service to God are placed side by side in the book of Deuteronomy:

> What does the Lord, your God, ask of you but . . . to love and serve the Lord, your God, with all your heart and all your soul, to keep the commandments and statutes of the Lord [10:12–13].

Obedience to the commandments was considered an inner *hearing* or surrender to God: "*Hear*, O Israel" (Deut. 6:4). This hearing meant imitation of God, "to follow His ways exactly" (Deut. 15:12) Most important was to imitate God's concern for the poor, the stranger, and the helpless:

> The Lord, your God . . . executes justice for the orphan and the widow, and befriends the alien, feeding and clothing him. So you too must befriend the alien, for you were once aliens in the land of Egypt [Deut. 10:17–20].

In the Sermon on the Mount, Matthew places the commands of Jesus side by side with God's commands: "You have heard it said to you . . . but I say to you." Just as obedience to God in the Old Testament is a direct personal service to God, so obedience to Jesus' commands is a direct personal service to Jesus *and* to God. This is why Jesus in the judgment scene can say, "I was hungry and you gave *me* to eat" (25:35). These words are the exact counterpart of Matthew 14:16, in which Jesus commands that the hungry be fed: "You yourselves give them to eat." The only difference is the substitution of "me" for "them," which indicates that service to the poor and hungry are service to Jesus himself. In Matthew 25:44 lack of response to the hungry, thirsty, naked, stranger, sick, and prisoner is equated with "not serving" Jesus.

We can sum up Matthew's viewpoint as follows: Instances of

serving the hungry, thirsty, poor, and sick, are much more than specific acts of kindness. They are part of the gospel itself, necessary responses to Jesus' command to feed the hungry. They are also direct personal service to Jesus himself, and likewise to God. They are part of faith that is an obedience and hearing in the deepest sense of opening up one's entire being to God's unconditional love and unlimited sensitivity for the needs of the poor and helpless.

LUKE, A GOSPEL OF BREAD

In the Acts of the Apostles and his Gospel, Luke is almost obsessed by the centrality of food and drink in the ministry of Jesus. In her joyful song of thanksgiving, Mary sums up God's goodness by saying, "to the hungry he has given every good thing" (Luke 1:53). Jesus is born in a manger, a feeding place for animals. Luke draws special attention to the deep significance of the manger (2:7, 12, 16). Jesus is the source of bread and nourishment for his people. Many people approached the fiery Baptist by the Jordan River asking what they should do to respond to the good news of the kingdom. John replied very simply, "Let the man with two coats give to him who has none. The man who has food should do the same (3:10–11).

In his opening sermon at Nazareth, Jesus recalls the story of the widow who shared her last remaining flour to provide bread for the prophet Elijah. As a result her flour jar never emptied during the years of famine (Luke 4:25; 1 Kings 17:7–16). In Luke's version of the Sermon on the Mount, Jesus emphasizes that the hungry will receive the greatest blessings of the kingdom: "Blessed are you who are hungry; you shall be filled." In juxtaposition he states, "Woe to you who are full; you shall go hungry" (7:20–25). Luke's version of the Lord's prayer stresses the necessity of providing bread for each person every day: "Give us *each day* our daily bread" (11:3).

The banquet theme in Luke contains important teachings on food and discipleship. Those who have a banquet should invite "beggars, the crippled, the lame, and the blind" instead of rich friends and relatives who will repay the hospitality with an invitation to their feasts (14:12–14). The kingdom of God is like a great banquet to which the whole world is invited (14:17–24). When the prodigal son is starving and desperate, he recalls there is abundant food in his father's house. When he arrives, a banquet celebration is prepared for him (15:17–24). A sharp contrast is drawn between the rich man eating sumptuously every day and Lazarus who is unable to obtain even the leftover morsels consumed by the dogs. In heaven the positions of Lazarus and the rich man are reversed (16:19–26).

The theme of sharing bread continues in the Acts of the Apostles, and Luke draws a number of close comparisons between Jesus' concern for the hungry and the role of the early church. One of these similarities has to do with feeding the hungry daily, the other with the relationship between food and discipleship. The members of the early Jerusalem community share bread together in their homes; many even sell houses and property in order to provide food for the needy (Acts 2:44–45; 4:33–34). Beyond that there is a daily distribution of bread and necessities for widows and other persons in need. The word that is translated as "daily" is the same as that used in Luke's version of the Lord's Prayer, as if to teach that we should pray to be able to provide each day for the needs of the hungry. Jesus' prayer, like the early church, emphasizes the daily necessity of food. At Jesus' command, the disciples distribute bread both during his ministry and later to the early church. In Luke's Gospel it is the twelve who come to Jesus to ask him to dismiss the crowds so they can seek food and shelter (9:13). Jesus' command to provide food is addressed directly to the twelve. It is they who direct the crowd to recline on the ground. At the end of the scene Luke alone makes the point of their exact obedience to Jesus: "They followed his instructions and got them all seated" (9:15). The Acts of the Apostles (6:1–6) states that until the number of followers became too great the disciples themselves distributed bread to the community, just as they had during Jesus' ministry.

When the pertinent passages in Matthew, Mark, and Luke are assembled and reviewed, there is no question that in these Gospels and in the Acts of the Apostles discipleship is closely connected to sharing food with the hungry. This concern also appears in John's version of the multiplication of the loaves. The Eucharist, a covenent to be a disciple of Jesus, links Christians to the instances of food sharing that are depicted in the Gospels. It also links us to the situation of hunger and exploitation that Jesus confronted during his ministry. Jesus lived in a world in which strong economic, social, religious, and political forces strove to exploit, impoverish, and deny sustenance to vast segments of the population. These forces strove to marginalize and segregate groups and individuals. Jesus resisted the temptation to use dominative power to combat those forces. However, one of the central biblical messages is that through discipleship to Jesus the exploitative forces can be overcome—the social barriers can be broken; those who are marginalized can receive their just share of the wealth of God's earth; the hungry can be fed.

PART II

THE EUCHARIST/
LAST SUPPER:
SACRAMENT AND ACTION-
SIGN OF THE KINGDOM

Introduction to Part II

Jesus' revolutionary proclamation was "good news for the poor." He did not come into this world to celebrate the status quo, but to initiate personal, social, and economic changes through effective action. During his earthly life he did not act alone but in and through a community dedicated to following him. After his death and resurrection, the Eucharist/Last Supper liturgy became the principal meeting place for Christians and a special external locus of the kingdom. Part 2 will study how the Eucharist is meant to continue and expand Jesus' mission of human liberation. It will emphasize the nature of the eucharistic meal as one of sharing with the hungry and poor. This will be intimately connected with the central meaning of the Eucharist as a sacrament and celebration of Jesus' death and resurrection.

Chapter 7

The Eucharist and Human Liberation

THE EUCHARIST AS ACTION-SIGN

In *The Eucharist and Human Liberation* Tissa Balasuriya describes the need for an action-centered liturgy:

> If Christian communities are to participate in the on-going revolutionary struggles for a better world, the liturgy must be related to them. The weekly gatherings for worship are the principal occasions when Christians meet. At present they are geared to action, but this is in connection with church-centered projects: church feasts, devotions, fund-raising for schools and social services, and the work of parish associations. The need is to link more seriously with the efforts of a people for their self-liberation from poverty, oppression, affluence, lack of freedom, and so forth [140].

In her book *The Eucharist and the Hunger of the World*, Monika Hellwig writes:

> The Eucharist is the assembling of people for an action. This action is supposed to make a difference, to bring about a change . . . . It is of crucial importance how we understand the change that it is supposed to effect [57].

This view is strengthened by her definition of a sacrament as a sign that gives grace. The Eucharist is a visible and outward sign

63

of grace because it represents "in a true sense the actions of Jesus himself" (57).

Writing on the effects of the Eucharist, St. Paul emphasizes that the one bread and one cup not only symbolize but effect true oneness:

> Is not the bread we break a sharing in the body of Christ?
> Because the loaf of bread is one, we, many though we are,
> become one body, for we all partake of the one loaf [1 Cor.
> 10:16–17].

The one bread makes believers one body in Christ because they share the inner dimension of this body, the Holy Spirit. Paul wrote that "it was in one Spirit that all of us, whether Jew or Greek, slave or free, were baptized into one body" (1 Cor. 12:13). We notice immediately in this text the compelling social implications. Elsewhere Paul states that this oneness in Christ radically affects the prevailing inequality between the sexes:

> All of you who have been baptized into Christ have clothed
> yourselves with him. There does not exist among you Jew or
> Greek, slave or freeman, male or female. All are one in
> Christ Jesus [Gal. 3:27–28].

In this text Paul writes about a visible body of Christ that is Christian community. Because it is one in Jesus it must reflect in action and behavior the equality demanded by the kingdom of God. The early Christian communities were small minorities with very limited political influence. Few of their members could even vote. The communities were limited in their impact on Greek and Roman societies in which patriarchal structures were strongly entrenched and in whose large cities more than half the population was composed of slaves. Yet those communities were challenged to act and did act. After two thousand years, though the status of the eucharistic community has changed in many ways, that community is still challenged to reflect in action the inner meaning of the Eucharist.

Closely linked to equality and oneness is the covenant nature of the Eucharist. It is indeed a pledge or covenant to be like Christ.

His death represented the ultimate step in his preaching and action concerning the kingdom of God. His death was voluntary—he made the decision to bring the Kingdom's good news for the oppressed and poor even to the nation's capital where the powerful, rich ruling class had the power to put him to death. When Christians share the bread and cup of the covenant, it is an outward sign of their commitment to the same justice that motivated Jesus. Jesus expressed his own commitment not only through words but by action. He confronted the rich oppressors among the priests by cleansing the Temple and by explaining his action to the people.

The Eucharist is also the celebration of Jesus' resurrection, which is God's own seal on Jesus' dedication to the kingdom and its demands for justice. The resurrection is one of many links between the word of God, with its emphasis upon justice, and the actions of Jesus and those who, in the past and today, wish to follow him. The word of God in scripture must retain its critical dimension by being fearlessly and rigorously applied to societies and their governments. By "critical" I do not mean destructive but rather judgmental and decisive. The word of God helps Christians make important decisions about action concerning justice in their societies. The church has the responsibility, especially in its proclamation of the word in the Eucharist, to maintain the critical stance of Jesus and the gospel. The resurrection and Eucharist are affirmations of that responsibility.

Yet the danger exists that a congregation will center its attention more on the outside world than on itself. The Christian community is a group that comes together primarily to critique the lives of its members. Paul reminds us of this in a very forceful manner when he writes, "What business is it of mine to judge outsiders? Is it not those inside the community you must judge? God will judge the others" (1 Cor. 5:12-13). The Christian community is not a select group of activitists for justice, peace, women's rights, or any other cause. Rather it is a community that comes together to critically search and examine its deficiencies in these and other areas. Because they have been the cause of much evil, members ask forgiveness from one another and from the poor and oppressed. The Christian community drinks the cup "for the forgiveness of sins" and pledges itself to renewed action so that it will not repeat its mistakes. It will live with understanding, compassion, and forgiveness yet with a determined stand. The spirit of the community should be like that of Paul, who wrote, "Help carry one another's burdens; in that way you will fulfill the law of Christ" (Gal. 6:2).

REJECTING DOMINATION: THE BREAD OF LOVING SERVICE

We have noted the contrast between the kingdom of Satan that is characterized by domination of others and the kingdom of God that is identified by loving service. Jesus brought about a revolution by renouncing domination and devoting himself to the service of the poor, oppressed, sick, and hungry. It is especially significant that Luke brings this entire matter into his description of Jesus' last supper. Luke does this to emphasize that these teachings must be understood by Christians when they gather for the breaking of bread.

The issue of dominative power and control is raised in Luke's account of the Lord's Supper. The power of the devil enters this holy atmosphere as Jesus warns Peter that Satan wants to sift him like wheat (22:31). Jesus' own view is revealed in a dispute, even in this solemn atmosphere, about dominating power and authority: "A dispute arose among them about who should be regarded as the greatest" (22:24). Jesus' words are addressed particularly to church leaders, represented by the twelve who are with him at the Last Supper (22:14). Jesus states that the greatest among them are those willing to be the least and the servants of others. They will sharply contrast with secular rulers who look for power, authority, and control over others. Jesus asks, "Who is in fact the greater; he who reclines at table or he who serves the meal? Is it not he who reclines at table?" (22:27). But Jesus answers his own question by choosing service as the way to overcome the kingdom of Satan that is based on power and control: "Yet I am in your midst as one who serves."

Luke's Acts of the Apostles shows that the twelve tried to take Jesus' directions literally. During the daily distribution of bread for the poor, they personally gave out provisions for the hungry and served them with their own hands (6:1–6). In addition, the twelve did not attempt to dominate the community. Important decisions affecting the church were not made individually by Peter or any of the twelve. The choice of a new apostle to take the place of Judas was made by a community selection of two candidates, one of whom was chosen after prayer and drawing lots (1:23–26). The important matter of food fellowship between Gentile and Jewish Christians was decided at a community meeting: "It was resolved by the apostles, and the presbyters, in agreement with the whole Jerusalem church" (15:22). The selection of seven Greek assistants to the twelve was made by the community (6:3–5). The members of the community prayed, reflected, and acted in unity—just as through the Eucharist they were collectively and individually made one with Christ.

Luke's account of the Last Supper and his descriptions of the functionings of the early Christian community highlight a number of themes: (1) in order to follow Jesus one must *serve* the "least"—the poor, the needy, the hungry; (2) real service involves direct participation in the process of relieving the suffering of others—the twelve personally handed bread to the poor; (3) certainly there must be leaders in the community, but they must eschew the use of power and avoid dominating and controlling the group's thinking and action; and (4) all members of the Christian community must collectively reflect on Jesus' actions and words and then convert that reflection into actions of sharing and service. The Eucharist infuses these themes into the Christian's life.

How can modern Christians and their communities apply these conclusions about Jesus and the early church? Tissa Balasuriya makes the following practical suggestion, based on his extensive experience in parish ministry, about how communities can begin to integrate the Eucharist and human liberation:

The liturgy should be reorganized to provide for personal and collective reflection on themes such as:

> *Food:* eating, fasting famine;
> *Clothing:* needs, cold, uses, fashions;
> *Shelter:* needs, slums and shanties, inequalities, remedies;
> *Family:* parent's days, father's day, mother's day,

women, children, youth, teenagers, the aged, the child, divorce, abortion, family planning;

Sex and Marriage: family life, women's rights;

Environment: pollution, waste, care of nature;

Health: disease, medicine, social services, doctors, nurses, world health (Good Samaritan):

Education: ignorance, needs, schools, universities, mass media, radio, TV, newspapers, books (Press Sunday);

Work: employment, unemployment, wages, conditions of work;

Leisure: availability, use, orientation, cinema, sports, music, arts;

Freedom: human personality development, independence day, love and service, church of service, disinterested charity;

Transport: needs (public, private), accidents, tourism;

Public Life: government, political parties, companies, corporations:

Truth: honesty and sincerity in public and private life, respect for truth from whatever source it comes;

Justice: social justice within the nation, capitalism, socialism, racial harmony, human rights;

Religious Harmony: wider ecumenism, tolerance, cooperation among religions, Christian unity, ecumenism (Unity Week), mission of the church;

Groups: workers' day (May 1st), farmers, industrialists, teachers, Pope's day, bishops, thanksgiving day;

World Justice: United Nations, UNCTAD, seas, action groups [Balasuriya, 136–37; on world justice see Corson-Finnerty].

The great obstacle to getting Christians to reflect and act upon these issues is the largeness and passivity of many modern congregations. To have the word of God engender decisions requires small groups in which each person has the opportunity for expression. It is not that large gatherings should be eliminated, but rather that they become much more effective through frequent, intimate gatherings where the word of God can be shared equally by all and where all have the opportunity for their own unique contribution.

Sometimes people in Christian groups lament that their leaders have taken over too much control and authority. However, this matter cannot be solved solely by criticism and complaints. It requires people to step in and assume the responsibilities of a follower of Jesus and not leave these tasks to others. In the ideals presented by Luke at the Last Supper, the real church leader is "one who serves at table"—one who is unique because *he or she* does not strive for dominative power but rather delights in the humble role of developing the talents and gifts of others so that they can be effective witnesses of the kingdom preached by Jesus. In this way real leaders make themselves "useless" by selflessly helping each person to be "useful."

Chapter 8

The Eucharist and the Meaning of Jesus' Death

The kingdom's inner resources, as exemplified in Jesus, are faith, prayer, and the Holy Spirit. These same inner resources are at the heart of the Eucharist/Last Supper liturgy. Without them we have nothing but meaningless ceremony.

The first of these, faith, is an openness or surrender to God in face of the impossible. This was the case of Abraham who believed God would give him a son despite the fact that he and his wife were very old. Jesus demanded faith from his disciples and from those who listened to his word. With faith, "nothing is impossible with God" (Luke 2:37). The Eucharist exemplified the summit of New Testament faith because it is the *Lord's* Supper. Christians gather together at the Eucharist in obedience to Jesus' word, and this obedience is called faith. They assemble not to socialize, witness a spectacle, or enjoy entertainment. They come together because they believe Jesus has risen, is still with them, and is still speaking to them. It is the risen Lord who is saying: "This is my body; this is my blood." The Eucharist has a radical dependence on this faith and is a very special occasion for the practice and deepening of faith.

Prayer is an expression of faith. Christians gather to pray for the coming of the kingdom of God in their lives and in their society, a goal that may often seem impossible to achieve. The Lord's Prayer is the central prayer of Christian worship. It is the great prayer for the concerns of the kingdom. All its petitions can be summed up in the words "thy kingdom come." In this phrase and in the Lord's Prayer in general the needs and the concerns of each individual and of the entire assembly are united. The prayer has a social dimension. One of the earliest directions for such prayer during the liturgy is found in 1 Timothy where the author writes:

> First of all, I urge that petitions, prayers, intercessions, and thanksgivings be offered for all men, especially for kings and those in authority, that we may be able to lead undisturbed and tranquil lives in perfect piety and dignity [2:1–4].

Although all persons can always express their needs privately, there is an extraordinary efficacy in the prayers of the whole community as the visible body of Christ. The power of such prayer is further enhanced by the conviction that it is the risen Christ who is uniting his prayers to those of the believers. Prayer and the Eucharist unite Christ and his followers in their struggle for a kingdom of justice. It is the risen Christ who is at the right hand of God and "who intercedes for us" (Rom. 8:34) in this struggle.

The third inner resource of the Eucharist is the Holy Spirit, through which union with the risen Jesus is achieved. This resource is highlighted in John's Gospel during Jesus' eucharistic discourse. Jesus proclaims that he is life-giving bread for the whole world:

> I am the living bread come down from heaven. If anyone eats of this bread he shall live for ever: the bread I will give is my flesh for the life of the world [6:31].

Although John's Gospel does not describe a eucharistic supper, Jesus' words reflect John's understanding of the inner meaning of the Supper of the Lord in the early church. The words "my flesh for the life of the world" almost duplicate Jesus' words in the other Gospels' narrations of the Last Supper. In the other Gospels, Jesus says, "This is my body," using the Greek word *soma*. In John, Jesus uses the Greek *sarx* which is a more literal translation of the semitic word for "flesh," the word that is used in Jesus' language to designate the body.

John then goes on to show that Jesus' words cannot be understood if they are only taken literally. The audience in his Gospel quarrels about the meaning of the words, saying, "How can he give us his flesh to eat?" (6:53). Jesus repeats his words, emphasizing and insisting upon their importance. However, even his disciples find them hard to accept, so Jesus explains that the words must be understood in terms of his risen body as an instrument and vehicle of the Holy Spirit. He says:

> What, then, if you were to see the Son of Man ascend to where he was before? . . . It is the spirit that gives life; the flesh is useless. The words I spoke to you are spirit and life [6:62].

These words explain that Jesus' statement about his "flesh for the life of the world" anticipate the rising of his Spirit-filled body, to which believers will be joined symbolically during the eucharistic meal. The special new strength of Christians will be an intimate communion through the Holy Spirit with the risen Jesus. This union will be so strong and deep that it will be like the union between Jesus and his Father. John's Gospel expresses this when Jesus says,

> The man who feeds on my flesh and drinks my blood remains in me, and I in him. Just as the Father who has life sent me and I have life because of the Father, so the man who feeds on me will have life because of me [6:56–57].

THE EUCHARIST AND JESUS' DEATH

For most of us death comes unexpectedly; we rarely choose or foresee it. For Jesus the chain of events leading to his death was not accidental, but deliberately chosen. He did not have to go to Jerusalem, nor did he have to remain there. He knew that Judas and the high priests were plotting his arrest, yet he chose to be faithful to his special call to preach his message of good news for the poor in the place where it was most needed. Jerusalem was the very place where the rich ruling classes and powerful leaders of institutional Judaism were most able to harm him, but it was also the place most in need of radical reform.

For Jesus death was the climax of his entire ministry. His willingness to face death proclaimed to the world that his announcement of the kingdom was more important than anything else, even his own life. His arrest, suffering, and death were a witness to the world of the priority of the kingdom with its hope for the poor and oppressed. Discipleship has its profoundest meaning when one goes so far as to risk death to show the world that self-interest has no part of a ministry of justice. The kingdom of Satan is dominated by self-concern and selfishness: life is preserved no matter what the cost in ideals and values. The supreme blow to Satan's kingdom is to be willing to die in the service of God's poor.

The decision to act in favor of the kingdom involves an extremely difficult personal struggle, and Jesus was not exempt from it. When he prayed before his arrest in the Garden of Olives, he went through a struggle that cost him sweat and blood. For a disciple there is no easy or short way. The way of the cross is the only option given by Jesus to his followers. Jesus said, ''If a man wishes to come after me, he must deny his very self, take up his cross, and follow in my steps'' (Mark 8:34). For this reason, the Gospels present Jesus' prayer in the Garden as a model of faith and obedience in the face of death. This model becomes clear when we examine the crisis before Jesus as he spent the night at the Mount of Olives. He was faced with an impossible situation. On the one hand, he knew that like the great prophets of the Old Testament, he must be obedient to the prophetic call to announce the good news in Jerusalem, the nation's capital. On the other hand, events in Jerusalem were fast moving toward his arrest and death. Judas, accompanied by soldiers from the high priests, may have already been approaching, ready to betray him. If his death came soon, how could he complete his urgent mission to announce the coming kingdom? Faced with this dilemma, Jesus was at first bewildered and uncertain what to do. He felt the need for a long period of intense prayer in order to form his decision and have the strength to carry it out.

Jesus searched the scriptures to find a parallel to his desperate situation. Finally he remembered the great Jewish model of obedience and sacrifice: Isaac, the son of Abraham. Here was a striking parallel to his own predicament. God had commanded that Isaac be sacrificed. This placed Abraham and Isaac in what seemed an impossible and illogical situation, for the continuance of Isaac's life was essential to fulfill God's promises for the future of Israel. Jesus recalled what Isaac said to Abraham. The words were directed also to God, for Abraham was acting in obedience to God's will. Isaac said to Abraham, "Abba" (the word, meaning "father," was used in the Aramaic translation), and his father replied, "Yes, son." Isaac continued, "Here are the fire and the wood, but where is the sheep for the holocaust?" (Gen. 22:7-8). Abraham answered, "God himself will provide the sheep for the holocaust." The author of Genesis then notes (as a sign of agreement) that they both continued on *together* toward the mountain of sacrifice.

With this image of Isaac in mind, Jesus prayed to his Father with the same feelings Isaac had had and with the same words that Isaac had directed to Abraham (see Grassi 1982). Jesus, like Isaac, pronounced the intimate family term, *Abba*. It was the affectionate expression of a dedicated son ready to obey his father's will no matter what the cost might be, even death. Jesus said, "Abba, Father, all things are possible to you; remove this cup from me; yet not what I will but what you will" (Mark 14:36). About an hour later Jesus returned to where Peter, James, and John had been praying. They were fast asleep. With a sad and weary heart Jesus awakened them and begged them to pray with him, saying, "Watch and pray that you do not enter into temptation; the spirit indeed is willing but the flesh is weak" (14:38). Then Jesus returned to prayer saying again and again the same words: "Abba, Father," and "thy will be done." Only after hours of agonizing prayer did Jesus finally make his decision. Then he stood up with new courage. He not only decided to stay on the Mount of Olives but even went forth willingly to meet his captors.

The Gospels place great emphasis upon this story because it is the last temptation and final crisis in Jesus' life. The word *Abba* sums up Jesus' whole attitude of obedience even as far as death. It also highlights the meaning of Jesus' faith: a complete surrender and openness to God even with the prospect of an excruciating death. Sacrifices have meaning only because they are God's will. Here was the most complete voluntary sacrifice, that of one's own life.

The Eucharist is a celebration and application of the meaning of Jesus' death, of his sacrifice. St. Paul tells the members of the early church that when they eat the Lord's Supper they "proclaim the death of the Lord until he comes" (1 Cor. 11:26). The baptismal *Abba* of the Christian is repeated again and again in the Eucharist as a celebration of Jesus' death. It is a commitment to go to the cross if necessary to establish the kingdom of God as the realm where the poor and oppressed receive God's special blessing and effective help. By means of the Holy Spirit the Christian achieves personal union with the risen Christ in the Eucharist and thereby receives the unlimited courage, strength, and energy needed to accomplish this "impossible" task despite all the opposition and obstacles that may stand in the way.

THE COSMIC EFFECTS OF THE DEATH/ SACRIFICE OF JESUS

Jesus' prayer, "Abba, Father" (Mark 14:36), was the supreme "yes" word of obedience to his Father's will. In this obedient "yes" we find the core meaning of sacrifice. In the biblical view sacrifice receives its power through an inner obedient gift of self, even if it involves the possibility of death. It is not the externals of the gift, even the loss of life, that are essential; the essential element is doing the action in conformity with God's will. The theme of this inner core of obedience is developed in Hebrews in a passage in which Jesus is portrayed as referring to lines in Psalm 40:

> Wherefore, on coming into the world, Jesus said: "Sacrifice and offering you did not desire, but a body you have prepared for me; holocausts and sin offerings you took no delight in. Then I said, 'As is written of me in the book, I have come to do your will, O God'" [10:5–8].

The author then explicates the psalm and applies it to Jesus' death. The "body" is the body of Christ. God wills the sacrifice, and thus Jesus' offering is an act that establishes God's will on earth; it is an acceptable sacrifice. The author writes: "By this 'will' we have been sanctified through the offering of the body of Jesus Christ one for all" (10:10). As a result, Jesus' sacrifice transcends the dimensions of time. He has become an eternal high priest with this continual offering of his obedient sacrifice to God.

In the Old Testament view, every sacrifice and every act of obedience was effective to the extent that it was an expression of a complete openness to God's will. It was effective because God in turn responded with an obedience that went far beyond anything achievable by human beings. The Hebrews considered the divine Spirit/breath/energy of God as filling the universe. Obedience and sacrifice brought about a certain "grounding" of the divine energy, so it was available in a superabundant fashion for human beings.

When this sacrifice or obedience went as far as death, there was no limit to God's response. When Abraham is about to sacrifice his son Isaac, God stops him at the last moment. God then responds with his own supreme, limitless gift:

> Because you have acted as you did in not withholding from me your beloved son, . . . I will bless you abundantly and make your descendants as countless as the stars in the sky and the sands of the seashore [Gen. 22:16–17].

The whole earth and the course of history is affected by this supreme act of obedience: "In your descendants all the nations of the earth shall find blessing—all because you obeyed my command" (22:18).

Although it has far greater meaning and effect, Jesus' sacrifice bears striking parallels to Abraham's willingness to sacrifice Isaac. An early Christian hymn quoted by St. Paul describes Christ as "obedient even to death" (Phil. 2:4). As God's response to Abraham's obedience is limitless, in the Philippians' hymn God responds with boundless power—Jesus is raised from the dead and is made lord of the universe:

> At Jesus' name every knee must bend in the heavens, on the earth, and under the earth, and every tongue proclaim to the glory of God the Father: Jesus Christ is Lord! [Phil. 2:11].

Like St. Paul, the evangelists emphasize the cosmic effects of the death of Jesus. They do this by describing the cosmic signs that take place at his death: the earthquake (Matt. 27:51), the darkening of the sun (Matt. 27:45; Mark 15:33), the tearing of the temple curtain before the Holy of Holies (Matt. 27:51; Mark 15:38), and so on. The temple veil guarded access to the holy Ark and, symbolically, the presence of God. No one but the high priest could enter, once a year, behind the veil of the Temple. The tearing of the veil symbolizes that complete access to God has now been opened through the one great sacrifice of Jesus.

This symbolism is explained in Hebrews:

> But when Christ came as high priest of the good things which have come to be, he entered once for all into the sanctuary, passing through the greater and more perfect tabernacle not made by hands, that is not belonging to this creation [9:11].

The text asserts that Christ was the real high priest, who entered not just behind the sacred veil but into heaven itself, which the Holy of Holies represented. In this way he made all of heaven's blessing and gifts available to the world.

St. Paul understood Christ's sacrifice not as an isolated action but as part of a great individual and community action by believers who constitute Christ's body. In Paul's letter to the Romans he challenges them to "offer your bodies as a living sacrifice holy and acceptable to God, your spiritual worship" (12:1). Paul writes in this fashion because he does not consider the risen Christ as someone separate and apart from the community. For him the risen Christ and believers are inseparable, forming a visible and tangible community. The inner bond that joins them is the Holy Spirit. This is why he writes, "It was in one Spirit that all of us, whether Jew or Greek, slave or free, were baptized into one body" (1 Cor. 12:13).

For Paul, the Holy Spirit has definite external social effects within groups of people: existing social and economic barriers are broken down. He writes, "The body is one and has many members, but all the members, many though they are, are one body; so it is with Christ" (1 Cor. 12:12). Consequently, the actions of the believers are also actions of the risen Christ, united to him in his one great sacrifice. The resurrection has achieved the tremendous effect of making the actions of the risen Christ become the actions of those who believe in him. In this way their actions are infused with a power and dynamism that they could not attain in isolation from Christ and the community of his followers. The eucharistic liturgy is the public expression of this power and a means to strengthen it again and again.

THE COSMIC EUCHARIST AND THE TRANSUBSTANTIATION OF THE UNIVERSE

In one sense the Eucharist is a public or exterior renewal of Christians' pledge to be disciples of Jesus. It also involves Christians' inner openness and obedience to God and is an inner link to God's boundless energy and strength. It is both spiritual and a pledge to action. We have noted that the key to the essential meaning of Jesus' death is found in his use of the word *abba*, in his total obedient "yes" to God. This "yes" to God, renewed for each Christian in the Eucharist, brought the gift of the Father to Jesus, and it brings that gift to each Christian and to the entire world.

The Gospel of John contains no description of the initiation of the Eucharist at the Last Supper. Behind this may be the author's conviction that Jesus' supreme obedience and sacrifice to God started the very moment he entered the world. For John, Jesus' death only brought this obedient behavior to a climax. Jesus' death was not an unusual act of obedience but part of the great act of obedience that was his whole life. John's Gospel explains this by emphasizing again and again Jesus' obedience to the will of his Father. Typical expressions are: "I did not come of my own will; it was he who sent me" (8:42); "it is not to do my own will that I have come down from heaven, but to do the will of him who sent me" (6:38; cf. also 4:34; 5:30; 6:39, 40).

In stressing Jesus' complete dedication to his Father's will, John's Gospel unfolds the inner secret of Jesus. A notable example of this occurs when the disciples leave an exhausted Jesus by a Samaritan well and go to the village to buy food to refresh themselves and the master. When they return, they urge Jesus to eat, saying: "Rabbi, eat something." But instead Jesus surprises them by answering, "I have food to eat of which you do not know" (4:32). The disciples naturally think someone else, perhaps the Samaritan woman, has brought him food. But Jesus explains, "Doing the will of him who sent me and bringing his work to completion is my food" (4:34).

The evangelist does not consider Jesus' actions in isolation from the community of his followers. Those united to him can share the same inner secret in all their actions: "The one who has faith in me will do the works that I do, and greater than these" (14:12). The inner secret and action are linked; faith and works are linked. This is what is signified in the phrases used in the title of this section. "Cosmic Eucharist" denotes that all our actions, united to those of Jesus in his supreme obedience to God, have a meaning and effect far beyond any immediate, perceptible results. Similarly, "transubstantiation of the universe" expressed the concept that Jesus' words and power are not to be restricted to the Last Supper or Eucharistic liturgy. Jesus' obedience to his Father's will reaches out in its effects to the whole universe. This bread of obedience is a mysterious food and energy that can transform all we do and bring deep changes in the world, especially in the people with whom we have immediate contact. There is no dichotomy between the spiritual effects of the Eucharist and the radical pledge of discipleship, a pledge that demands action to further the kingdom of justice on earth. Both share the same roots. The kingdom of God, good news for the poor, and all that pertains to it are *the will* of God. Both are side by side in the Lord's Prayer: "Thy kingdom come; thy will be done."

The task seems overpowering. We often feel very much alone and powerless before acute injustice and oppression. It is encouraging that Jesus himself felt that way but was able to draw on new sources of hope and energy. This hidden source of strength was his dedication to his Father's will, expressed through his "Abba, Father." The believer can tap into these same mysterious powerful roots. These roots reach down into the great inner binding power of the universe itself: the creative action of God. Obedience and openness to this makes available an endless source of unlimited energy that can be applied toward the quest to make the kingdom of God a reality.

This radical obedience is rooted in the will and is interior by its very nature. Yet Jesus expressed this publicly and verbally at the Last Supper. In doing so, he underscored that the Eucharist is a public expression of individuals' and communities' obedience to God, and he asked his disciples and all his followers to share the great inner secret that made his death a supreme and unlimited offering to God. Jesus symbolized this sharing by offering the disciples the covenantal cup that they could drink and share with him. In the Eucharist, Jesus offers all his followers this opportunity for obedience and discipleship. As with Jesus, this obedience is an interior dedication and act of the will. Frequent private renewal is needed. For many centuries Christian piety has expressed this in a "morning offering" or prayer that could be repeated often during the day. This offering is private, and yet at the same time united to its public expression in the Eucharist and the one eternal offering of Christ the high priest.

In the early church, the Lord's Prayer was the great link between the public Last Supper liturgy and the interior prayer of each Christian. It is found in the earliest known liturgy from the *Didache* or Teaching (of the twelve apostles), written around the middle of the second century. The *Didache* directs each Christian to pray the Our Father three times each day (8:3).

The Lord's Prayer is the most suitable offering because it is Jesus' own prayer with its kingdom-centered petitions. It is also suitable because of a number of ancient connections between it and the Eucharist: In Matthew, Mark, and Luke, the petitions in the Lord's Prayer are closely linked to the Last Supper. They are found in Jesus' prayer in the garden that immediately follows the supper. In addition, the simple words "our Father" contain beneath them the precious "abba" of Jesus. They sum up for Christians a renewal of the "abba" expressed in their baptismal commitment, and the Lord's Prayer thus links the interior prayer of each Christian with the Eucharist, with a public proclamation to do God's will and act to further the kingdom of justice. In chapter 6 of the Acts of the Apostles, Luke connects the daily bread of the Lord's Prayer with the daily distribution of food for the hungry. The Eucharist and social action are intertwined.

Through the Eucharist, Christians are linked not only to Jesus' life but also to his death and resurrection. The Eucharist has more than spiritual or interior effects—it gives Christians access to God, to the source of energy and strength upon which Jesus drew throughout his life but particularly in the days immediately preceding and following the Last Supper. In the face of his own death, Jesus instituted the Eucharist at the Last Supper, thus binding his followers in discipleship to continue his mission to bring good news to the poor. Because the Eucharist connects Christians with God's will and Jesus' obedience, Christians' actions to further the kingdom of justice take on profound and widespread meaning and effect. Through the Eucharist, Christians are linked to Jesus' option to lovingly serve the poor and hungry—that bond is a call to them to act to promote justice and feed the hungry.

Chapter 9

The Eucharist and Bread
for a Hungry World:
Principles and Action

On the most fundamental level the Eucharist is a sharing of food. Monika Hellwig writes

> The simple, central action of the Eucharist is the sharing of food—not only eating but sharing. The simple, central human experience for the understanding of this action is hunger. However, the experience of hunger, which we all share, should not be simply taken for granted and allowed to slide out of focus in the action [Hellwig, 10].

The way this sharing is done and the meaning attached to it have enormous consequences because it is an action performed by hundreds of millions of people on our globe each week.

In the conclusion of his book *The Lord's Table: Eucharist and Passover in Early Christianity,* G. Feeley-Harnik points out that *food-language* was the basic way Christianity was understood in the ancient world and was the reason it had such a deep impact:

> Food seems to have been regarded as the most accessible, the best way of introducing ordinary mortals to the ineffable wisdom of God, and perhaps also the best way of tran-

scending the babel of tongues in which early Christians
found themselves [166].

Feeley-Harnik emphasizes that the Eucharist, unlike the Jewish
Passover, *was not a family meal* (144). The Old Testament regula-
tions carefully prescribed that each family should have a lamb for
its household (Exod. 12:4). However, Jesus celebrated his Last
Supper not with his family but with his disciples. Jesus' relationship with them constituted a new solidarity that transcended family bonds and sometimes even opposed them. Jesus' sharing of
bread and wine was an effective symbol that *every* man and
woman could be brother and sister and thus share together the
earth's resources. Closely connected to this is the food-language
announcing that Christians are a covenantal community pledged
to work together to continue the ministry of Jesus to the poor. It is
a community coming together for a definite action, an action to
bring about change.

THE WORLD'S FOOD-LANGUAGE

What is the world's food-language? Jack A. Nelson's *Hunger
for Justice: The Politics of Food and Faith* offers a profound
analysis. Nelson argues that food has become the principal
economic and political weapon of leading nations, especially the
United States. One of the ways he illustrates this is by listing the
far-reaching effects of Public Law 480 (the Agricultural Trade
Development and Assistance Act of 1954), a program of "surplus
agricultural disposal policies." In Nelson's words, through this
program the United States was able to do the following:

- profitably dispose of harmful surpluses and bail out the
  U.S. economy,
- create future markets by undermining local food producers and encouraging production of agricultural prod-
  ucts for export based on the principle of comparative
  advantage,
- make optimal use of poor countries as consumers of U.S.
  agricultural and industrial goods,

- encourage poor nations to abandon policies directed toward self-reliance and to integrate their economies into the international free-enterprise system,
- facilitate U.S. corporate expansion abroad through Cooley loans,
- fund counterinsurgency and other military efforts that protect U.S. political and economic interests,
- and finally, foster poor-country indebtedness and dependency [24–25].

Sales of food and military weapons have become interwoven and have increased. Nelson points out that during the 1972 trade deficit "two 'solutions' soon emerged to the impending crisis: a massive campaign to sell weapons abroad and food sales to a world experiencing shortages the United States had helped create" (90).

The horrible specter of world hunger is not due to overpopulation but to patterns of land and food distribution. A prime example of this is India, where, as Nelson points out,

An estimated 50 percent of the land is owned by 8 percent of the people and 70 percent of India's farmers have less than one acre. Absentee landlords and moneylenders are powerful groups in the countryside. Landless peasants pay high rents, borrow money, and receive pitifully low wages. . . . India's agricultural production is organized in a manner that serves the interests of a small group of people at the expense of a vast majority. Large numbers of children thus become the only basis for old age security. In striking contrast, in neighboring China with over one billion population, men and women retire at 60 and 55 respectively with 70 percent of their previous wages [123].

Food has become more and more an affair of big business. It is estimated that 5 percent of the farmers in the United States now control over one half of the nation's farm lands. The eight largest oil companies own sixty-five million acres of land. Nelson states, "Within our capitalist economy, land has become a commodity to be traded, an opportunity for investment, and no longer a public trust'' (156). The results of all this are shocking and appalling:

> Millions of our children grow up believing that the origin of
> food is the supermarket. They, and many of us as well, no
> longer appreciate the delicate interface between creation,
> soil, and human labor. This interface, which is known as
> agriculture, has been rapidly replaced by agribusiness. With
> the onslaught of agribusiness has come violence to ourselves
> and our soil. Ours is literally a throw-away society, and we
> throw farmers off the land and replace them with chemicals
> and machines as easily as we dispose of nonreturnable bot-
> tles and cans [Nelson, 155].

THE EARLY CHURCH AS A MODEL
FOR A NEW FOOD-LANGUAGE

We are confronted by an enormous, overpowering, and con-
fusing Tower of Babel that has been created by the world's food-
language. To overcome this confusion, the Christian today must
recover the revolutionary food-language that is expressed in the
fundamental meaning of the Eucharist. As has been proven in
previous chapters, there is a profound connection between discipleship and feeding the hungry. Now it is important to understand the link between the Eucharist and food sharing in the early
church.

In the earliest New Testament description of the Eucharist
(written about A.D. 56), we find that Paul writes to the Corin-
thians about an agape meal or food sharing that preceded the
celebration of the Lord's Supper. Paul had received shocking
news from Corinth about the way the Lord's Supper was being
celebrated: "First of all: I hear that when you gather for a meeting
there are divisions among you, and I am inclined to believe it" (1
Cor. 11:18). These divisions or cliques were groups of people who
shared a common meal as a prelude to the celebration of the
Lord's Supper. They did so in accord with their social or
economic status. Many wealthy Christians sought out friends of
similar status and shared sumptuous food and drink with them.

Thus the rich and poor ate in a glaringly different fashion. So Paul writes:

> When you assemble it is not to eat the Lord's Supper, for everyone is in haste to eat his own supper. One person is hungry while another gets drunk. . . . Would you show contempt for the Church of God and embarrass those who have nothing? [11:20–22].

To emphasize his point, Paul recalls the Last Supper of Jesus as an example of sharing and love—even in the face of betrayal:

> The Lord Jesus on the night in which he was betrayed took bread, and after he had given thanks, broke it and said, "This is my body which is for you" [11:23–24].

Paul is convinced that eating Christ's body is an intimate sharing and that the communicants become one body:

> Is not the bread we break a sharing in the body of Christ? Because the loaf of bread is one, we, many though we are, are one body, for we all partake of the one loaf [10:17].

In Paul's view becoming one body implies a serious responsibility to brothers and sisters who are poor or needy. Thus before eating a person "should examine himself first; only then should he eat of the bread and drink of the cup" (11:28). This warning is given because a special sign of members of the body of Christ is love and concern for those who are suffering and in need. Paul compares the interdependency of the communicants with the body and writes, "If one member suffers, all the members suffer with it" (12:26).

Paul's concerns were not only for sharing within the local community; they also extended to people in need in distant places. Paul recognized the very special needs of poverty-striken Jewish communities in Judea. Despite the distance and ancient racial rivalry, he asked the Gentile churches in Greece and elsewhere to make a collection every Sunday that could be brought to Jerusalem:

> About the collection for the saints, follow the instructions I
> gave to the churches of Galatia. On the first day of each
> week everyone should put aside whatever he has been able to
> save, so that the collection will not have to be taken up after
> I arrive [16:1].

The motivation behind such a collection was to promote true fellowship and equality based on sharing:

> Your plenty at the present time should supply their need so
> that their surplus may one day supply your need, with equal-
> ity as the result [2 Cor. 8:13–14].

Paul believed that only a new food-language that promoted equality and sharing could make possible a unification of Jews and Gentiles. Furthermore, it could make the ideal of sufficient bread for the world community a reality.

The Gospels also point out the connection between the Eucharist and food sharing in the early church. The most striking support of this is found in the accounts of the multiplication of loaves: Jesus' distribution of the loaves is described in the same words that are used to describe the Last Supper, which was already a liturgical celebration in the churches by the time the Gospels were written. Matthew's description of the Last Supper has, "Jesus took bread, blessed it, broke it, and gave it to his disciples" (26:26). The account of the feeding of the five thousand contains the same sequence and description: Jesus took up the five loaves and two fish and "blessed and broke them and gave the loaves to his disciples" (14:19). Luke's Gospel and Acts of the Apostles draw even tighter connections between food distribution and the Eucharist. Luke injects a number of details to connect the multiplication of loaves with the Eucharist and food distribution in the early church (see chap. 6 above). The evangelist makes the eucharistic connections even more explicit by paralleling the multiplication of the loaves to a meal which two disciples share with the risen Jesus on the road to Emmaus (Luke 24:13-31). In this story the two disciples press a mysterious stranger (Jesus in disguise) to stay with them at an inn to receive hospitality. Then Jesus repeats the same sequence of actions that is described in the accounts of the Last Supper and the multiplication of loaves: he blesses the bread, breaks it, and distributes it to them (24:30). Then the disciples recognize Jesus in the *breaking of the bread,* and he disappears from their midst. It is interesting that in the accounts of both the multiplication of the loaves (see Luke 9:12) and the Emmaus incident, the sharing of bread and the sharing of hospitality are found together.

The links between the "breaking of the bread" and food for the hungry continue in the Acts of the Apostles. In Acts 2:42, Luke notes that the early Jerusalem Christians "devoted themselves to the apostles' instruction and the common life, to the breaking of bread and prayers." While there is no direct eucharistic reference, this breaking of bread is connected with the apostles' instructions and prayers. It is not an ordinary family meal, but a meal that is eaten by disciples and that has special meaning. This meal appears closely connected to sharing food with the hungry, for in the next verse (2:44) it is mentioned that the members of the early community shared all things in common; many sold lands, houses, and possessions so there would be enough food and necessities for everyone. Elsewhere Luke does mention the breaking of bread with a direct eucharistic connotation. In Acts 20:7, Luke describes a Christian gathering on the first day of the week (Sunday) for the breaking of bread.

The Lord's Prayer, with its petition "give us this day our daily bread," was closely linked with the Eucharist in the early church. So it is quite significant that Luke's version of this petition: "Give us *each day* our daily bread" (11:3) uses the exact words, *each day* to describe the distribution of bread for the poor in the Jerusalem community (Acts 6:1).

In addition to the biblical texts, there are a number of sources that contain significant descriptions of and comments upon the sharing of food and possessions among the members of the early church. One of these is the *Didache,* written in the second century, which contains an instruction on two ways: there is the way of life and the way of death. The sharing of material things is found in the way of life and is intimately connected with the sharing of spiritual gifts:

> Do not turn away from the needy but share all with your brother and do not claim that it is your own. For if you are sharers in immortal things, how much more in mortal [4:8].

The prayers connected with the common meal, which have some eucharistic features, contain a strong emphasis on the role of God as creator and source of food and nourishment for everyone:

> Thou, Lord Almighty, has created all things for Thy name's sake and hast given food and drink to men for their refreshment, so that they might render thanks to Thee; but upon us Thou hast bestowed spiritual food and drink, and life everlasting through Thy Son [10:3].

The members of the *Didache* community retained the Old Testament custom of tithing, first for their prophets and then for the poor:

> Take all the first-fruits of the winepress and of the harvest, of the cattle and of the sheep, and give them to the prophets, for they are your high priests. But, if you have not a prophet, give it to the poor. If you make bread, take the first share and give according to the commandment [13:3–5].

In his *Apologia,* composed around A.D. 150, St. Justin Martyr writes to non-Christians about Christian practices. He wants them to know that the Christian Sunday liturgy promotes equality between rich and poor through the sharing that takes place in the common meal. He describes the sharing of material goods that takes place in connection with the Eucharist:

> The wealthy, if they wish, contribute whatever they desire, and the collection is placed in the custody of the president. With it he helps the orphans and widows, those who are needy because of sickness or any other reason, and the captives and strangers in our midst; in short, he takes care of all those in need [chap. 67].

This mutual sharing through a common fund is considered to be one of the remarkable changes that comes about when a person becomes a Christian:

> We who loved above all else the ways of acquiring riches and possessions now hand over to a community fund what we possess, and share it with every needy person [chap. 14].

A strong emphasis is placed on God as creator of the world whose resources are to be shared by all:

> The rich among us come to the aid of the poor and we always stay together: For all the favors we enjoy we bless the Creator of all, through His Son Jesus Christ and through the Holy Spirit. . . . Sunday, indeed, is the day on which we all hold our common assembly because it is the first day on which God, transforming the darkness and matter, created the world; and our Savior Jesus Christ arose from the dead on the same day [chap. 67].

In the middle of the third century, St. Cyprian made an emphatic statement about the connection between the Eucharist and sharing with the poor and hungry. He wrote:

> You are rich and wealthy and imagine that you celebrate the Lord's Supper without taking part in the offering. You come to the Lord's house with nothing to offer, suppressing the part of the sacrifice which belongs to the poor [15].

TODAY'S EUCHARIST: TOWARD A NEW FOOD-LANGUAGE FOR THE WORLD

What can we do to change the powerful food-language responsible for so much global suffering and oppression? How does this suffering and oppression relate to the realities of churches or parishes in the United States? Even in the richest country in the world shocking hunger and poverty often exist within a few miles of affluent churches. These contrasts remind us that worldwide ten thousand people die of starvation each week, despite the fact that there is sufficient food to feed them.

We are challenged to find effective ways to make connections between the Eucharist, the bread of life, and food for the hungry: ways that are meaningful and personal, as well as effective and concrete. There are no easy solutions. We cannot return to the first-century church where smaller memberships made possible an effective daily table at which food was shared with the hungry.

However, there are important steps that can be taken to make every church or parish a vital learning center where the new food-language of the Eucharist is effectively taught. The first step is to establish a church "hunger committee" so that the question of local and world hunger will be a permanent community concern and an urgent priority. The function of such a committee is primarily educational, but it should also point out and initiate practical ways to connect the table of the Lord's Supper with the table of the hungry both locally and internationally. Appendix A lists a number of resources that such a committee can use for effective education and action.

The second step is for the hunger committee to plan and organize effective ways to involve the whole community in the process of raising its consciousness about hunger and the problems related to it. The committee might organize hunger liturgies, especially during Advent and Lent. The entire liturgy—readings, prayers, sermon—can be effectively used to link the table of the Lord with the tables of the hungry, poor, and oppressed (see Simon for helpful materials related to such liturgies).

In addition, the liturgy should be action-oriented. The committee can distribute cards so that parishioners can sign up for various projects in connection with the needs of the hungry. Tables can be set up in the church so people can have easy access to written materials, pamphlets, brochures, and so forth that are available through the organizations listed in appendix A. Tables with writing materials, envelopes, and lists of names and addresses can be arranged so that people will be encouraged to write the White House or their representatives in the Senate, House, or state government on matters related to hunger issues.

Workshops devoted to hunger issues can be organized periodically. A number of the organizations listed in the appendix can supply speakers, films, and presentations that address these issues. During Lent, church members can be invited to a soup dinner followed by a talk and discussion on matters related to hunger education. The soup dinner can be the occasion for a request of funds for hunger projects that have come to the attention of the hunger committee through its sources of information.

The third and most essential step is to develop an ongoing concern for the hungry that expresses itself in concrete action on the part of individuals and the community. It should be something in which every family can take part and something with which even children can identify. There is a danger in sporadic efforts, such as a fund-raising soup dinner every Lent. If help to the hungry is limited to such efforts, the false impression is given that the acute needs of the hungry and starving can be taken care of by a donation once or twice a year. Painful hunger is a daily occurence that must be countered by ongoing effective programs that enter into the lives of every Christian.

THE NEW FOOD-LANGUAGE OF THE EUCHARIST: FEEDING THE HUNGRY

A second-century church document suggests a way to unite prayer, worship, fasting, and help for the hungry:

> On the day of your fast . . . compute the total expense for the food you would have eaten on the day on which you intended to keep a fast and give it to a widow, an orphan, or someone in need. . . . If you perform your fast, then, in the way I have just commanded, your sacrifice will be acceptable in the sight of God. . . . A service so performed is beautiful, joyous, and acceptable in the sight of the Lord [Hermas, Shepherd of, 5.3.7–8].

Today a growing number of churches and individuals have adapted the ancient advice of the Shepherd of Hermas and have incorporated it in a very practical way into their liturgies and lives through various programs. An example is Skip-a-Meal, a very popular program in Santa Clara County, California. Participants pledge to fast one meal each week, unite this with prayers for the hungry, and give their savings through this fasting to buy food for the hungry. Their offerings are brought to the altar, usually on one Sunday a month, where they are united to the offering of Christ himself, who was so identified with the hungry that he said, "I was hungry and you gave me to eat" (Matt. 25:35). Several thousand families from various churches in the Santa Clara area have formed their own hunger committees and independently, through volunteers, administer the Skip-a-Meal program. All participants, whether an individual or a church, select the group or agency, local or international, through which their offering will go to buy food for the hungry.

Along with fasting for the hungry, there is a program of prayer and education. The daily prayer serves a double purpose: it is a renewal of a basic commitment to the kingdom of justice on earth, a kingdom in which hunger and starvation will be eliminated; and the prayer is a means to express concern and bring help to the hungry. The education takes the form of a monthly newsletter sent to all participants to remind them of social and political means to bring about effective action to help the hungry on the local, state, and national levels.

These are but a few examples of the expression of an effective new food-language that is being created through meaningful celebration of the Eucharist. New languages cannot be used in isolation; they must spread until they are used all over the world. That is why organization is so important—beginning from grassroot levels. What one or two people do has an impact, but what one or two million Christian congregations do can break down the old Tower of Babel with its dominant food-language.

This new food-language is not just words but a total commitment to bring hunger to an end on our globe. The language has an essential nonverbal component in the breaking of bread with the hungry. But there is also a verbal element to private and public prayer. Furthermore, the language is visibly active when men and women gather to take definite political and economic action to counter the prevailing world food-language. The new food-language does not simply relieve symptoms but fights to implement the fundamental solution to the problem: that people in the middle and upper classes must have less so that others may have more, the patterns of food distribution must change. Fasting from food and the voluntary experience of hunger is a decisive pledge and a first step, but many further steps must be taken to-

ward more effective understanding and action. Fasting is also
part of a personal education progress that involves learning to do
without many things that have gradually become "necessities."

Jesus, of course, fasted, and he experienced hunger. He knew
what it was to be hungry and poor, and his ministry was one of
loving service to the poor and oppressed. His ministry was not
purely spiritual. He came to bring change in the political,
economic, and social structure of first-century Palestine. The Eucharist is a renewal of the covenantal relationship Christians have
with Jesus. It is a renewal of our pledge of discipleship to him. To
be a disciple of Christ means to imitate him—it means to struggle
for structural change in our societies and to be obedient to the
Father, the God of justice. The twelve and many members of the
early church were prototypes of this discipleship: the members of
the early church shared their food and possessions with the needy;
the twelve personally distributed food to those who were without
sufficent provisions. So too must we, as disciples, serve the poor,
the needy, the hungry, the oppressed. The dynamic meaning of
the Eucharist as a new food-language for the world can challenge
each one of us to make crucial decisions to change our lifestyles
and to imitate Jesus in initiating effective political and social action that will decisively effect the world and feed the hungry.

Appendix A

Resources for Hunger Committees in Local Churches

The following is a list of groups and sources that might be of use to local committees:

1. Bread for the World, 6411 Chillum Pl., NW, Washington, DC 20012. The group was founded by Eugene Carson Blake. Arthur Simon, author of *Bread for the World*, is also an active member. The organization has a lobby in Washington to promote hunger-related legislation. To be more effective, it is organized in chapters throughout the U.S. Individual or group members receive an informative newsletter so communities and churches can be alert to supporting political action on hunger-related issues.

2. Institute for Food and Development Policy, Box 40403, San Francisco, CA 96110. The organization was started by Frances Moore Lappé and Joseph Collins, coauthors of *Food First*. The institute carries on research and food education as well as advocacy of political and social programs to aid the hungry.

3. American Freedom from Hunger Foundation, 1625 I Street, NW, Washington, DC 20006. This group originally began as a liaison between the U.S. and the UN Food and Agricultural Organization. It sponsors education programs and seminars on hunger. It has played an important role in organizing U.S. support and participation in several worldwide food gatherings.

4. The American Friends Service Committee, 1501 Cherry St., Philadelphia, PA 19102. It has a hunger education program and supports development and relief programs in more than twenty countries. It publishes a regular, informative newsletter.

95

5. CARE, 660 First Ave., New York, NY 10016. CARE began after World War II as a relief organization. It now focuses on the Third World and provides self-help assistance, medical service, and training. It has a supplemental food program that feeds over twenty million people daily.

6. Catholic Relief Services, 1011 First Ave., New York, NY 10022. The organization has a very effective lenten education and support program. Its representatives are found in most of the developing nations. It not only provides emergency help for the hungry but has developed a large number of self-help programs.

7. Church World Service, 475 Riverside Dr., New York, NY 10015. This is an interdenominational Christian program. It develops and funds programs to help the poor and needy worldwide. Programs include emergency food assistance, disaster aid, grassroots development programs, health services, children's programs, and educational services.

8. CROP, Elkhart, IN 46515. This is a special project of Church World Service. It has undertaken fund raising for the hungry through fasts, hunger walks, marathons, and workshops. It has helped farmers and others to make direct donations of wheat, food, and even animals to needy people all over the world.

9. Oxfam-America, Box 288, 302 Columbus Ave., Back Bay Station, Boston, MA 02116. This group specializes in projects that promote self-help and development in several countries, including Peru and Bangladesh. Oxfam depends on personal donations, which it channels to programs that help develop local initiative to counter the problems of hunger and poverty.

10. World Hunger Education Service, 1317 G. St., NW, Washington DC 20005. This is an information and consultation center that publishes a regular newsnote entitled *Hunger Notes*. It sponsors special seminars in Washington, DC, for persons who want to learn more about problems related to hunger and how to go about working to solve them.

Appendix B

Modern Statements by Christian Churches on the Problem of Hunger

THE CATHOLIC CHURCH

Joseph Gremillion has collected and commented upon Catholic statements made since the time of Pope John XXIII on hunger and social justice. A summary of these teachings is given by Suzanne Toton in her book on world hunger and Christian education (102–21).

In *The Church in the Modern World,* Vatican II made a broad statement on hunger in view of God's purpose in creation to make all the earth's resources available to all humanity.

> For the rest, the right to have a share of earthly goods sufficient for oneself and one's family belongs to everyone. The Fathers and Doctors of the Church held this view, teaching that men are obliged to come to the relief of the poor, and to do so not merely out of their superfluous goods. If a person is in extreme necessity, he has the right to take from the riches of others what he himself needs. Since there are so many people in this world afflicted with hunger, this sacred Council urges all, both individuals and governments, to remember the saying of the Fathers: "Feed the man dying of hunger, because if you have not fed him you have killed him." According to their ability, let all individuals and governments undertake a genuine sharing of their goods. Let them use these goods especially to provide individuals and nations with the means for helping and developing themselves [no. 69, in Abbot].

97

However, even before Vatican II, Pope John in his encyclical *Mater et magistra* (1961) had already given impetus to such a statement by his views on the urgency of the hunger problem:

> Perhaps the most pressing question of our day concerns the relationship between economically advanced commonwealths and those that are in the process of development. The former enjoy the conveniences of life; the latter experience dire poverty. Yet, today men are so intimately associated in all parts of the world that they feel, as it were, as if they are members of one and the same household. Therefore the nations that enjoy a sufficiency and abundance of everything may not overlook the plight of other nations whose citizens experience such domestic problems that they are all but overcome by poverty and hunger, and are not able to enjoy basic human rights. This is all the more so, inasmuch as countries each day seem to become more dependent on each other. Consequently, it is not easy for them to keep the peace advantageously if excessive imbalances exist in their economic and social conditions.
>
> Mindful of our role of universal father, we think it opportune to stress here what we have stated in another connection: "We all share the responsibility for the fact that populations are undernourished. Therefore, it is necessary to arouse a sense of responsibility in individuals and generally, especially among those more blessed with this world's goods" [nos. 157–58, in Gremillion].

Two years later, in *Pacem in terris,* Pope John saw the responsibility for hunger as having to do with the rights and duties existing among persons:

> It is not enough, for example, to acknowledge and respect every man's right to the means of subsistence. One must also strive to insure that he actually has enough in the way of food and nourishment [no. 32, in Gremillion].

During and after Vatican II, Pope Paul VI continued to emphasize the crisis of world hunger and point to solutions that could be brought about through social justice, especially in regard to the developing Third World. He began his encyclical *Populorum progressio* with the following words:

> The development of peoples has the Church's close attention, particularly the development of those people who are striving to es-

cape from hunger, misery, endemic diseases, and ignorance; of those who are looking for a wider share in the benefits of civilization and a more active improvement of their human qualities; of those who are aiming purposefully at their complete fulfilment . . . . Today the peoples in hunger are making a dramatic appeal to the peoples blessed with abundance. The church shudders at this cry of anguish and calls each one to give a loving response of charity to this brother's cry for help [nos. 1–3, In Gremillion].

As one practical way to meet the challenge of world hunger, Pope Paul in the same document suggested the establishment of a world fund:

At Bombay We called for the establishment of a great *World Fund,* to be made up of part of the money spent on arms, to relieve the most destitute of this world. What is true of the immediate struggle against want, holds good also when there is a question of development. Only world-wide collaboration, of which a common fund would be both means and symbol, will succeed in overcoming vain rivalries and in establishing a fruitful and peaceful exchange between peoples [no. 51].

In its summary document, *Justice in the World,* the second general assembly of the Synod of Bishops (1971) repeated Pope Paul's request for a general fund and then made the request more specific:

We feel that we must point out in a special way the need for some fund to provide sufficient food and protein for the real mental and physical development of children [no. 68, in Gremillion].

The address of Pope Paul VI to the World Food Conference (see Gremillion, pp. 599–606) held in Rome in 1974 constitutes the most specific response to the problems of world hunger ever drawn by Rome. For this reason important excerpts from this document are reprinted below:

We are happy to greet you, the participants at the World Food Conference assembled in Rome under the auspices of the United Nations. There is no need to tell you that we share intensely in your preoccupations, for our mission is to carry on the teaching and activity of the Master from whom the sight of a hungry crowd prompted the moving exclamation: "I feel sorry for all these people; they . . . have nothing to eat. I do not want to send them off hungry, they might collapse on the way" (Mt 15:32).

1. The documentation prepared by your Conference describes the various aspects of hunger and of malnutrition, uncovers their causes and attempts to foresee their consequences, by recourse to statistics, market research and indices of production and consumption. In their accuracy, these indications take on a tragic eloquence: but what is it like then to come face to face, on the spot, with the realities that they represent? Recent disasters of every kind—drought, floods, wars—immediately give rise to pathetic cases of food scarcity. In a less spectacular but equally painful way, all are faced by the hardship created in the deprived classes by the rise in the cost of foodstuffs, which is a sign of their impending scarcity, and by the ever more marked lessening of international aid—given in the form of foodstuffs—which had powerfully contributed to the rehabilitation and progress of peoples after the last war.

Lack of proper nourishment has long-term and sometimes unforeseeable effects. It has serious consequences on future generations and presents ecological and health hazards which cause damage to populations, more deep-seated than the maladies immediately apparent. It is truly painful to come to such a realization and to admit that, up to now, society seems incapable of tackling world hunger, although unprecedented technical progress has been achieved in all spheres of production. This is the case, for example, in regard to fertilizers and mechanization, and in regard to distribution and transport. A very few years ago, in fact, it was hoped that in one way or another the rapidity of the transmission of information and of goods, as well as the technological advances achieved, would be able speedily to eliminate the dangers of the ancient scourge of famine afflicting for a long period a nation or a whole region. That these hopes have not been realized explains the grave atmosphere surrounding your work. Hence also comes the hope mingled with anxiety with which the peoples of the world are watching your work . . . .

2. The threat of hunger and the burden of malnutrition are not an inevitable destiny. In this crisis nature is not unfaithful to man. Its productive capacity, on land and in the seas, remains immense and is still largely unexploited. While on the one hand fifty percent of arable land has, according to the generally accepted view, not yet been put to use, on the other hand we are faced by the scandal of enormous surpluses of foodstuffs that certain countries periodically destroy, because of the lack of a wise economy which would have guaranteed the useful employment of these surpluses. Here

we have merely illustrations of a fact which no one challenges in its stark reality, even if some doubt whether it is possible to draw quickly enough from this potential what is needed to allay the hunger of expanding mankind. And when we speak of "allaying hunger" we are all in agreement that it is a question of more than just prolonging a minimal and subhuman biological existence. What is in question is "to provide each man with enough to live— to live a truly human life, to be capable by his own work of guaranteeing the upkeep of his family and to be able through the exercise of his intelligence to share in the common goods of society by a commitment freely agreed to and by an activity voluntarily assumed" (Speech to FAO, 16 November 1970: AAS 62 [1070], p. 831). It is of course with a view to this level of life that you have drawn up the calculations of your reports, according to which a campaign capable of feeding expanding mankind is possible on a technical level, but demands considerable effort.

3. The present crisis appears in fact above all to be a crisis of civilization and of solidarity. A crisis of civilization and of method, which shows itself when the development of life in society is faced from a onesided point of view, and when only the model of society that leads to an industrialized civilization is considered, that is to say, when too much confidence is placed in the automatic nature of purely technical solutions, while fundamental human values are forgotten. It is a crisis that shows itself when the accent is placed on the quest for mere economic success deriving from the large profits of industry, with a consequential almost total abandonment of the agricultural sector, and the accompanying neglect of its highest human and spiritual values. It is also a crisis of solidarity, a crisis that sustains and sometimes accelerates the imbalances between individuals, groups and peoples, a crisis that is unfortunately the result—as is increasingly evident—of the insufficient willingness to contribute to a better distribution of available resources, especially to the countries that are less well provided for and to the sections of mankind that live essentially on an agriculture which is still primitive.

We thus touch upon the paradox of the present situation: mankind has at its disposal an unequalled mastery of the universe. It has means capable of making the resources of the universe yield their full potential. Will those who possess these means remain as though struck by paralysis when confronted with the absurdity of a situation in which the wealth of some can tolerate the enduring poverty of so many? Or a situation in which the highly enriched and diversified food consumption of some peoples can be satisfied at seeing the minimum necessary for existence doled out to all the others? Or a situation in which human intelligence could come to the aid of so many people afflicted by sickness, and yet evade the task of ensuring an adequate nourishment for the most defenceless sectors of mankind?

4. One could not have arrived at that point without having committed serious errors of orientation, even if sometimes only through negligence or omission. It is indeed time to find out where the mechanisms have broken down, so that the situation can be corrected, or rather reordered from beginning to end. The right to satisfy one's hunger must finally be recognized for everyone, according to the specific requirements of his age and activity. This right is based on the fact that all the goods of the earth are destined primarily for universal use and for the subsistence of all men, before any individual appropriation. Christ based the judgment of each human being on respect for this right (cf. Mt 25:31 ff.) . . . .

We have spoken of the quantity of food necessary for the life of each and every man. But the problem of quality is equally important and also depends on an economic choice. In this matter the most industrialized nations are particularly concerned. In an atmosphere which is becoming polluted and in the face of the frenzied rush to create artificial substitutes, capable of quicker production, how shall we manage prudently to safeguard healthy nourishment with no serious risk for the health of the consumers, especially children and young people? And how, in these same nations, can we break with a consumption which is excessive because of the rich abundance of foodstuffs, which proves to be damaging to those concerned and which leaves others unprovided for? In this field too the situation calls for vigilance and courage.

5. Other observations concern the flow of the resources which would allow the present situation to be remedied. All are agreed that multilateral and bilateral aid to the agricultural sector has been notoriously insufficient. In preparation for your Conference great care has been taken to list the requirements which would be entailed by the intensification of food production in the developing countries, by the drawing up of policies and programmes aimed at improving nutrition, and by measures for strengthening world food security . . . .

6. But the most widespread international aid, the increased tempo of research and of the application of agrarian technology and the most detailed planning of food production will have little effect unless one of the most serious gaps in technical civilization is

filled as quickly as possible. The world food crises will not be solved without the participation of the agricultural workers, and this cannot be complete and fruitful without a radical revision of the underestimation by the modern world of the importance of agriculture. For agriculture is easily subordinated to the immediate interests of other sectors of the economy, even in countries which at present are trying to initiate the process of growth and economic autonomy . . . .

It is the dignity of those who work on the land, of all those engaged in different levels of research and action in the field of agricultural development, which must be unceasingly proclaimed and promoted. We said as much when we received the FAO Conference in 1971: "It is no longer sufficient to stem the growing distortion of the situation of the members of the rural community in the modern world; it is necessary to make them an integral part of it in such a way that coming generations will no longer experience this debilitating feeling of being left aside, of being on the sidelines of modern progress where improvement is concerned" (AAS 63 [1971], p. 877).

This will be achieved through a worldwide and balanced process of development supported by a political desire on the part of governments to give agriculture its rightful place. It is a question of putting an end to the pressure of the stronger economic sectors—a pressure which is stripping the countryside of those very energies which would be able to ensure high productivity in agriculture. There must be established a policy which will guarantee to the young people of rural areas the fundamental personal right to a deliberate choice of a worthwhile profession, equal both in conditions and advantages to what only the exodus to the city and industry seems able to guarantee them today.

7. Without any doubt, here again the reforms will have value only if individuals adapt themselves to them. That is why education and training have a fundamental role to play, by ensuring the proper preparation is not lacking. "The collaboration of the rural population is necessary; . . . agricultural workers must be faithful to the profession which they have chosen and which they value; . . . let them follow the programmes of cultural improvement which are essential if agriculture is to break out of its rooted and empirical immobility and adopt new forms of work, new machines, new methods" (Address to Italian Agricultural Workers, 13 November 1966: *L'Osservatore Romano,* 14-15 November 1966).

What is especially important therefore to those afflicted with hunger is that governments should offer all agricultural workers the chance to learn how to cultivate the land, how to improve soils, how to avoid diseases in farm animals and how to increase yield. It is also important finally that, within the framework of an adequate preparation, agricultural workers should be granted the credit they need. In a word, it is necessary to give to the members of the farming community responsibility in their production and progress. Thus we find ourselves brought back to the notion of integral development embracing the whole man and all men. For our part we have never ceased to exhort humanity to work towards this goal.

8. These are the thoughts which we offer you as our contribution to your work. They come from the awareness that we have of our pastoral duty and they are inspired by confidence in God who neglects none of his children, and by confidence in man, created in God's image and capable of accomplishing wonders of intelligence and of goodness. Faced with the hungry crowds, the Lord did not content himself with expressing his compassion. He gave his disciples a command: ''Give them something to eat yourselves'' (Mt 14:16), and his power came to the aid only of their helplessness, not of their selfishness. This episode of the multiplication of the loaves then, contains many lessons that are applicable in view of the grave needs of the present moment. Today we wish primarily to re-echo this call to effective action. We must envisage the creation, on a long-term basis, of the possibility, for each people, of accurately ensuring its subsistence in the most suitable way. Nor must we forget in the immediate future to remedy, by sharing, the urgent needs that are experienced by a great part of mankind. Action must be united to charity.

This progressive reorientation of production and distribution also involves an effort which must not be simply a constraint imposed by fear of want, but also a positive will not to waste thoughtlessly the goods which must be for everyone's benefit. After freely feeding the crowds, the Lord told his disciples—the Gospel relates—to gather up what was left over, lest anything should be lost (cf. Jn 6:12). What an excellent lesson in thrift—in the finest and fullest meaning of the term—for our age, given as it is to wastefulness! It carries with it the condemnation of a whole concept of society wherein consumption tends to become an end in itself, with contempt for the needy, and to the detriment, in the end, of those very people who believed themselves to be its beneficiaries, having become incapable of perceiving that man is called to a higher destiny.

Pope John Paul II has echoed the statements of popes and bishops who preceded him. During his visit to the United States in October 1979, he delivered a homily to a gathering of over eighty thousand people at Yankee Stadium in New York City. His special theme was peace and social justice. With special reference to hunger and poverty he said:

> Social thinking and social practice inspired by the Gospel must always be marked by a special sensitivity toward those who are most in distress, those who are extremely poor, those suffering from all the physical, mental and moral ills that afflict humanity, including hunger, neglect, unemployment and despair.

Using the gospel parable of the rich man and Lazarus, he applied its teaching to social consciousness in these words:

> All of humanity must think of the parable of the rich man and the beggar. Humanity must translate it into contemporary terms, in terms of economy and politics, in terms of all human rights, in terms of relations between the "first," "second" and "third world." We cannot stand idly by when thousands of human beings are dying of hunger. Nor can we remain indifferent when the rights of the human spirit are trampled upon, when violence is done to the human conscience in matters of truth, religion and cultural creativity [John Paul II].

THE PROTESTANT CHURCHES

The Protestant Churches do not have one person or group that speaks officially for all of them. To get a real picture of Protestant response to the world hunger crisis we would have to gather together statements from hundreds of widely scattered groups—which would of course fill many volumes. For a summary of the direction of modern Protestant response to questions of social justice there is the excellent book by Paul Bock, *In Search of a Responsible World Society*.

Most of the larger Protestant denominations belong to the World Council of Churches. The council's general and specific assemblies produce statements, of course, but these are in no way binding for particular churches. They represent the views of the participants, not the views of all Protestant churches. The council's statements on hunger, like those made by the Catholic church, are brief because hunger is not viewed as a separate problem but as intertwined with all the difficulties and problems that are encountered in trying to form "a responsible society." These last words formed the theme of the first world assembly of the World Council of Churches at Amsterdam in 1948. The assembly generated the following definition:

> A responsible society is one where freedom is the freedom of men who acknowledge responsibility to justice and public order, and where those who hold political authority or economic power are responsible for its exercise to God and the people whose welfare is affected by it . . . It is required that economic justice and provision of equality of opportunity be established for all members of society [cited in Lefever, 14].

In preparation for the next world assembly of the World Council of Churches in Evanston Illinois, in 1954, a special conference was held in Lucknow, India, so the "responsible society" could be better understood in view of the Asian experience. The conference declared:

> For us as Christians in East Asia a society is responsible when (1) social justice is actively promoted, (2) full development of natural resources is pursued, (3) the fullest share possible of the national wealth is guaranteed to all, (4) human rights and freedoms are effectively guaranteed, (5) the people have full sovereignty for their own affairs, (6) the principles of social and political life are in accordance with the concept of man as a person called to a responsible existence in community [cited in Bock, 73].

The Evanston assembly took up the suggestions of the Lucknow conference in the preparation of a document on "The Responsible Society in World Perspective."

The third international assembly of the World Council of Churches took place in New Delhi in 1961. With increased Third World membership, there were many challenges from representatives to work more specifically for social justice in the developing countries. The assembly approved the report of the section that had devoted itself to the topic of "Service." The report contained the following statement:

> The Christian is not afraid of change, for he knows how heavy are the burdens of poverty and privation carried today by the majority of mankind. He is ready to initiate changes and forward reforms that serve the ends of justice and freedom, that break the chains of poverty; and is willing to cooperate with all who share his concern for the welfare of mankind. . . . In the specific field of economic

development, we welcome the vigorous effort to increase production and raise living standards. In much of the world the basic needs of man for food, clothing, shelter and health remain unmet or are constantly endangered. There are areas of particular frustration remaining static in the midst of surrounding progress. There are countries where economic progress has been slow or erratic, because the demands of the people seem to be endless. Thus a strategy of development is overdue, and though it can be undertaken only by concerted inter-governmental action, part of our service— as producers, consumers or taxpayers—lies in our willingness to share with others, and to subordinate our personal, group or national interest to the well-being of all [*The New Delhi Report,* 94–95].

The whole assembly at New Delhi also approved the report of the Committee on the Division of Inter-Church Aid, Refugee, and World Service. Prominent in the committee's report was the call for the establishment of interchurch aid as an instrument of service:

Such action includes refugee service, relief work, the meeting of emergencies through natural, political or social disasters, and aid in finding a lasting solution to the problems of poverty, disease, hunger, under-employment and unemployment [*The New Delhi Report,* 230].

The major theme of the fourth assembly, held at Uppsala, Sweden, in 1968, was development. Major speakers in the plenary sessions called upon the assembly to give attention to the plight of the poor, who form more than half of the human family. The speakers challenged the churches to wage war against mass poverty, along with economic and social injustice. One section was devoted entirely to the topic "World Economic and Social Development." The section's final document challenged Christians to develop a real sense of solidarity with those in need throughout the world:

The great majority of men and also of Christians are aware of their responsibility for members of their own national societies who are in need. But few have discovered that we now live in a world in which people in need in all parts of the world are our neighbors for whom we bear responsibility [cited in Toton, 119].

The section on "Dynamics and Development" pointed out that real justice could be obtained only through fundamental institutional change in the developing as well as developed countries, that is, in the international economy:

> It is necessary to instill social and economic processes with a new dynamic of human solidarity and justice. In several developing nations ruling groups monopolize the produce of their economy and all foreign resources to aid and abet them in such action. In the international economy, the amount received as aid is often neutralized by inequitable patterns of trade, excessive returns on private investment, and the burden of debt repayment [cited in Toton, 119].

The fifth world assembly of the World Council of Churches was held in Nairobi, Kenya, in 1976. The theme was "Jesus Christ Frees and Unites." Liberation theology was a powerful influence in this assembly. There were two sections on liberation: "Education for Liberation and Community" and "Structures of Injustice and Struggles for Liberation." In his analysis of this assembly Ernest Lefever writes:

> Nairobi proclaimed that poverty, racism, violation of human rights, and militarism . . . the world over result from unjust systems foisted upon humanity by the white-dominated consumer societies of the Northern Hemisphere. "Liberation" meant changing or overthrowing unjust structures and replacing them with systems that serve rather than exploit people. Fundamental human rights included 'the right to work, to adequate food, to guaranteed health care, to decent housing, and to education for the full development of the human potential" [43].

The section on "Structures of Injustice and Struggles for Liberation" issued a very powerful document inspired by the best of liberation theology. It begins with this statement:

> Structures of injustice and struggles of liberation pose a formidable challenge to the Church today. In striving to meet it, the Church has no other foundation on which to stand than it has in Jesus Christ. From him it has received its mandate: to witness to the truth which judges and to proclaim the good news which brings about freedom and salvation. In seeking its particular place in today's struggles for social justice and human liberation, the Church needs to be constantly guided by its divine mandate . . . . Whenever a Christian is confronted by structures of injustice and takes part in struggles for liberation, he or she is bound to expe-

rience the grip of destructive forces which are at work throughout the human family. Such forces give a taste of the "principalities and powers" of which Paul spoke [cited in Paton, 100–101].

The theme of the sixth assembly, held in Vancouver in 1983, was "Jesus Christ: The Life of the World." A preparatory document was issued in April 1982 by the Latin American members of the World Council of Churches. The document contains a section entitled "Evidence of Signs of Death" which makes the following statement about the connection between the arms race and hunger and poverty in the world:

> Another extremely paradoxical fact, in a continent of so much want and distress, is the intensification of the arms race: 75 percent of the arms exports of the industrialized countries go to the Third World. Such military expenditures involve an enormous waste of financial and human resources, raw materials, science and research, resources which could be used to improve the life of millions of poor and needy. Between 1965 and 1975, the number of men under arms in Latin America rose from 780,000 to almost one million [*Ecumenical Review*, 394].

Another important preparatory report for the 1983 assembly was that of the consultation of "Ecumenical Perspectives on Political Ethics" held in Cyprus in October 1981. The report made a strong statement on the political dimensions of the gospel:

> Because the churches are part of the political reality, they cannot escape their accountability in the exercise of their own role within that reality. The gospel has an inescapable political dimension which manifests itself most clearly where it is proclaimed under conditions of extreme oppression. There the Bible sustains and inspires the oppressed; the Bible can even become a subversive book in the eyes of the oppressor. This is due to the clear bias in the biblical witness in favour of the oppressed, the poor, those under domination and without power [*Ecumenical Review*, 409–10].

The Vancouver assembly generated a document entitled "International Food Disorder." The following are excerpts from that significant document:

> 1. The scandal of hunger calls for the immediate attention of the churches. Estimates are that at a minimum there are 400 million people in the world who do not receive adequate sustenance of

food. Many die for lack of food; many more suffer from diseases and disabilities caused by insufficient or unbalanced diet. It is often children who are the victims of malnutrition and who are deprived of the possibility of fullness of life . . . .

3. There has been in recent years a significant increase in world food production but starvation and malnutrition are at a crisis level in many countries due to the inability of the rural and urban poor to produce or purchase food. The present international food disorder is rooted in mismanagement of food resources. The current misuse of natural resources also calls for attention to the problems which may arise in providing adequate food for future generations.

4. The present patterns of production and distribution of food have led to a serious disorder in the international food markets. Many countries of the South produce food which is often insufficient for a balanced diet for their people. They are therefore forced to buy from the world market and to depend on external food aid. Much of their agricultural production is aimed at and therefore dependent on markets of the wealthier nations. The agricultural infrastructure, research and finance are often aimed at improving the production of crops for export, rather than producing food which can be consumed by the people of the producing countries. At the same time, industrialized countries are seeking to reduce production levels on their land so that prices for their crops will continue to rise.

5. Food has also been used in international affairs as a political weapon for bargaining among nations and within nations. Where persons or nations have been perceived to be unfriendly or strategically unimportant, food has often been denied. We emphasize that food must not be used as a political weapon. Every person has a fundamental and unconditional human right to adequate food. Furthermore, every nation has the right to self-determination and self-reliance, and under no circumstances should food supplies be used to control or limit that right.

6. The development of technologies of food production, which require the use of chemical inputs, has in certain instances hampered food production in the developing countries which have received chemicals banned as unfit for use in the industrially developed world. It is critical that the distribution of unsafe chemicals be halted and that education about the use of chemical substances be provided for farming communities.

7. The causes of the food disorder are also located within na-

tions. In many countries, in both industrialized and developing nations, much of the productive land is controlled by large land owners and transnational corporations who exploit the land and do not allow the farmers, peasants, and landless rural workers to participate in making decisions which would benefit them. As a result, not only are small farmers often forced off their land or reduced to poverty. In addition, efficient transportation and marketing of food for domestic consumption are often lacking. Within many countries both land reform and reorientation of agricultural research, extension, infrastructure and marketing to serve the interests of peasant farmers are urgently needed if the growth of rural and urban malnutrition is to be halted and reversed.

8. Related to these concerns about the policies of food production and distribution is the effect of these policies on the natural resources of the earth. Natural calamities have been exacerbated by the mismanagement of resources. The problems which hamper food production today and which cause grave concern for the future include not only soil erosion, deforestation, drought, ineffective water conservation and irrigation systems, but also the under-utilization of land and human resources, sometimes due to war and refugee crises. In addition, unequal land allocation and resettlement of refugees sometimes result in over-utilization of land reducing its long-term potential.

9. The Sixth Assembly of the WCC, meeting in Vancouver, Canada, in 1983, has as its theme, "Jesus Christ—the Life of the World." We believe that this theme calls us to respond urgently to the international food disorder.

10. The reality of hunger reminds us of the many biblical accounts which link one's response to Christ with a response to the hungry of the world. To feed or not to feed them is indeed to do likewise to Christ (Matt. 25:35, 42). Through the miracle of the feeding of the five thousand, Jesus showed his disciples that by his will there could be ample food to feed the hungry (John 6:1–14); and in this context he said, "I am the bread of life" (John 6:35). During this Assembly we have celebrated the gift of life in its fullness, the eucharistic life to which Jesus calls his Church. The ecumenical text on "Baptism, Eucharist, and Ministry" reminds us that "the eucharistic celebration demands reconciliation and sharing among all those regarded as brothers and sisters in the one family of God, and is a constant challenge in the search for appropriate relationships in social, economic and political life" (Eucharist, D. 20).

11. We believe that food is a gift from God which through human labor serves for the sustenance of life in its fullness. The ordinance of the jubilee year in Leviticus 25 reminds us that the life sustaining resources of the world as gifts from God are to be distributed justly among all people and redistributed regularly to allow for self-reliance of all.

12. We are called to confession today. The fact that so many are hungry shows that we have failed to be faithful and responsible stewards of God's creation.

13. We call upon member churches to take action to redress the international food disorder by:

    a. Strengthening ecumenical structures for meeting emergency and short-term food needs.

    b. Building ecumenical support for long-term solutions to the problem of hunger through appropriate policies, including increased access to land and to work for rural and urban poor, husbanding and renewing of natural resources, greater self-reliance in basic food production and more equitable structures of international trade in agricultural products.

    c. Continuing education programs on the causes of hunger and the international food disorder.

    d. Monitoring policies of governments, international agencies and transnational corporations regarding food production, distribution and land reform.

    e. Developing programs of advocacy and support for the participation of the poor in the production of food and in the distribution of food resources.

    f. Recognizing and encouraging specific programs of international aid for agricultural research in support of the production of food for consumption by the people of the producing country.

    g. Engaging in more generous and effective sharing within congregations and communities as well as nationally and internationally of resources relevant to the provision of food and to the ability to produce it.

    h. Supporting efforts for peace and justice and human rights which will counteract the forces which divert resources from production and just distribution of food.

    i. Taking leadership in preparing for the future, working with the scientific community to ensure that the causes of the international food disorder will be addressed in any technological developments.

j. Being advocates for communities and movements of farmers and landless rural workers.

k. Denouncing current policies that the International Monetary Fund imposes on nations in debt, which result in the reduction of food available to the poor, thereby increasing malnutrition, hunger-related diseases and infant mortality.

l. Investigating and taking action on the investments of church funds and use of church land so that they support agricultural and rural development in which people participate fully.

m. Supporting churches and movements which are working to alleviate the effects and causes of hunger in various nations and communities throughout the world.

Works Cited

Abbott, Walter, ed. 1966. *The Documents of Vatican II.* New York: Guild Press.

Avila, Rafael. 1981. *Worship and Politics.* Maryknoll, N.Y.: Orbis Books.

Balasuriya, Tissa. 1979. *The Eucharist and Human Liberation.* Maryknoll, N.Y.: Orbis Books.

Bock, Paul. 1974. *In Search of a Responsible Society: The Social Teachings of the World Council of Churches.* Philadelphia: Westminster Press.

Cassidy, Richard J. 1978. *Jesus, Politics and Society.* Maryknoll, N.Y.: Orbis Books.

Corson-Finnerty, Adam. 1982. *World Citizen: Action for Global Justice.* Maryknoll, N.Y.: Orbis Books.

Cyprian, St. *De opere et eleemosynis.*

Didache. 1947. In *The Apostolic Fathers.* Translated by Joseph Marique. The Fathers of the Church series. New York: CIMA Publishing Co.

Ecumenical Review (Geneva). 1982. No. 34.

Feeley-Harnick, G. 1981. *The Lord's Table: Eucharist and Passover in Early Christianity.* Philadelphia: University of Pennsylvania Press.

Galilea, Segundo. 1981. *Following Jesus.* Maryknoll, N.Y.: Orbis Books.

Grassi, Joseph A. 1978 (Oct.) "You Yourselves Give Them to Eat." *Bible Today.* Pp. 1704–9.

———1981. "'I was Hungry and You Gave Me to Eat': The Divine Identification Ethic in Matthew." *Biblical Theology Bulletin.* 11:81–84.

———1982 (Sept.). "Abba, Father (Mark 14:36): Another Approach." *American Academy of Religion Journal.* Pp. 450–58.

Gremillion, Joseph, comp. 1976. *The Gospel of Peace and Justice: Catholic Social Teaching since Pope John.* Maryknoll, N.Y.: Orbis Books.

Hellwig, Monika K. 1976. *The Eucharist and the Hunger of the World.* New York: Paulist Press.

115

Hermas, Shepherd of. 1947. *Parables*. In *The Apostolic Fathers*. Translated by Joseph Marique. The Fathers of the Church series. New York CIMA Publishing Co.

John Paul II, Pope. 1980. "Homily at Yankee Stadium." *Catholic Mind*. 78:19–24.

Johnson, Luke. 1981. *Sharing Possessions, Mandate and Symbol of Faith*. Philadelphia: Fortress Press.

Josephus, Flavius. 1974. *Antiquities*. In *Complete Works of Flavius Josephus*. Translated by William Whiston. Grand Rapids, Mich.: Kregel.

Justin Martyr, St. 1948. *The First Apology*. In *The Writings of Saint Justin Martyr*. Translated by Thomas Falls. The Fathers of the Church series. New York: Christian Heritage.

Lappé, Frances Moore, and Joseph Collins. 1977. *Food First*. Boston: Houghton Mifflin.

Lefever, Ernest W. 1979. *Amsterdam to Nairobi: The World Council of Churches and the Third World*. Washington, D.C.: Ethics and Public Policy Center, Georgetown University.

Montefiore, H. W. 1962. "Revolt in the Desert?" *New Testament Studies*. 8:135–41.

Munro, Winsome. 1982. "Women Disciples in Mark." *Catholic Biblical Quarterly*. 44:225–41.

Nelson, Jack A. 1980. *Hunger for Justice: The Politics of Food and Faith*. Maryknoll, N.Y.: Orbis Books.

Neusner, Jacob. 1971. *From Politics to Piety*. New York: Prentice Hall.

The New Delhi Report: The Third Assembly of the World Council of Churches. 1962, New York: Association Press.

Nolan, Albert. 1978. *Jesus before Christianity*. Maryknoll, N.Y.: Orbis Books.

Paton, David M., ed. 1976. *Breaking Barriers: Nairobi, 1975*. Grand Rapids: Eerdmans.

Rhoads, David M. 1976. *Israel in Revolution 6–74 C.E.* Philadelphia: Fortress Press.

Roth, C. 1960. "The Cleansing of the Temple and Zechariah." *Novum Testamentum*. 4:174–81.

Simon, Arthur. 1975. *Bread for the World*. New York: Paulist Press.

Toton, Suzanne C. 1982. *World Hunger: The Responsibility of Christian Education*. Maryknoll, N.Y.: Orbis Books. Part 1 of this work contains a study of the causes of world hunger.